The Long Conversation

IE Business Publishing

IE Business Publishing and Palgrave Macmillan have launched a collection of high-quality books in the areas of Business and Management, Economics and Finance. This important series is characterized by innovative ideas and theories, entrepreneurial perspectives, academic rigor and practical approaches which will make these books invaluable to the business professional, scholar and student alike.

IE Business School is one of the world's leading institutions dedicated to educating business leaders. Palgrave Macmillan, part of Macmillan Group, has been serving the learning and professional sector for more than 160 years.

The series, put together by these eminent international partners, will enable executives, students, management scholars and professionals worldwide to have access to the most valuable information and critical new arguments and theories in the fields of Business and Management, Economics and Finance from the leading experts at IE Business School

The Long Conversation

Maximizing Business Value from Information Technology Investment

Oswaldo Lorenzo
Professor of Management, IE Business School, Spain

Peter Kawalek
Professor of Information Systems,
Manchester Business School, UK

Gastón González
Expertia Consulting Group

Boumediene Ramdani
Senior Lecturer in Strategy and Operations Management,
Bristol Business School, UK

First published 2011 by
PALGRAVE MACMILLAN

Palgrave Macmillan in the UK is an imprint of Macmillan Publishers Limited, registered in England, company number 785998, of Houndmills, Basingstoke, Hampshire RG21 6XS.

Palgrave Macmillan in the US is a division of St Martin's Press LLC, 175 Fifth Avenue, New York, NY 10010.

Palgrave Macmillan is the global academic imprint of the above companies and has companies and representatives throughout the world.

Palgrave® and Macmillan® are registered trademarks in the United States, the United Kingdom, Europe and other countries.

ISBN: 978–0–230–29788–3

This book is printed on paper suitable for recycling and made from fully managed and sustained forest sources. Logging, pulping and manufacturing processes are expected to conform to the environmental regulations of the country of origin.

A catalogue record for this book is available from the British Library.

A catalog record for this book is available from the Library of Congress.

10 9 8 7 6 5 4 3 2 1
20 19 18 17 16 15 14 13 12 11

Transferred to Digital Printing in 2015

CONTENTS

TABLES

Figures

BOXES

It takes a long time

For the last 20 years, companies have been adopting and implementing enterprise systems (ES). These represent the large-scale information technology (IT) systems of today, providing a backbone for many organizations worldwide. ES are so significant in scope and complexity that we can call them platforms. These platforms underpin both individual businesses and the supply chains between them. The implementation of these platforms has to be done with clear strategic and operational aims: to automate transactions, reduce costs, increase customer satisfaction, integrate with suppliers and ultimately make better decisions. And yet, companies find this experience of implementing ES not as they initially anticipated. Projects are harder, business cases are more difficult and the learning process is much, much longer. Despite this, at the end of everything, they enter a new reality, one in which the potential benefits are greater than they had foreseen.

Why is this happening? And what do firms do to ensure that they get value from their investment in technology? These are the two questions that prompted a ten-year research program by four academics based in Spain, the UK and Latin America. Their journey was frustrating and enlightening at the same time. But in the end, the data pointed to a simple and unequivocal conclusion. It is a conclusion that may not be fashionable – but should, nevertheless, be music to the ears of CEOs everywhere.

The reality is that it takes a long time and a lot of learning to get the best out of your ES. In the current world economic situation some people say we need more new IT, more tools to change our ways. But we disagree with this argument. What businesses really need now is to stop looking for the next technology silver bullet and make the most of what they already have. In short, businesses need to maximize the value of their existing IT assets.

To succeed in the coming years, companies must continue and intensify what we call "the Long Conversation" – the strategic and operational dialogues that businesses began years ago. Companies do not need to acquire the latest hardware and/or software, but they do need new organizational practices, new capabilities and new social networks to support the continuity of that conversation. Learning and then innovation follow from this and one day, inevitably, there follows a whole new platform. But for now, the focus is on learning and adapting.

The research

This book is based on ten years of empirical research with companies in Europe, Latin America and Asia. It also includes data and examples of companies in which we have been working as consultants and experts. The application of the findings from this longitudinal study into the companies advised has been a way to test the ideas and insights developed academically.

The empirical study started ten years ago with the study of three Latin American companies: a coffee company, an engineering company and a chemical company. Later, we added two organizations in the UK (a brewery and a charity); one in Asia (a machine company); and a global ES project in an IT company. More recently, we were involved in a study of a European telecom company that was adapting its ES to support a more centralized business model. The findings of this research have been published in an article in the *California Management Review*[1] – entitled "The Long Conversation" – and other academic journals and conferences such as the Communication of Association for Information Systems, Information and Management, The European Conference in Information Systems and the Americas Conference in Information Systems.[2] But the results have not yet been translated for practitioners.

We have applied these findings in companies worldwide in sectors such as banking, government, manufacturing, media and high-tech industry. The book will also include detailed evidence drawn from some of these consulting experiences.

The Brewery Company

Brewery is a multinational, famous brand beer company. It operates in 150 countries and employs more than 40,000 people. The company is among the five largest brewing companies in the world. The beer portfolio includes hundreds of brands. They vary significantly in volume, price, target audience and geographic penetration. This brand portfolio includes well-known international brands and strong local brands. This study took place in the UK at two sites, including the implementation of functionality such as financial, assets management, materials management, logistics, human resources and executive information systems.

The Charity Institution

This institution is one of the largest independent charity organizations in the UK and Republic of Ireland with a board of volunteer trustees. Its turnover is in excess of £100 million. Volunteers are at the heart of this institution. They rely on more than 40,000 volunteers. Training volunteers is one of its critical processes to ensure that their mission is achieved. From its foundation, the institution has saved thousands of lives. The study took place at the UK headquarters and included the implementation of financial, human resources and executive information systems.

The Chemical Company

This company is in the chemical distribution business in Latin America. It operates distribution facilities and sales service centers in six cities. The company has a turnover of US$20 million. Bulk liquid storages are maintained at the country's main ports for receipt of import parcels. The company sells a broad range of high-value additives and chemicals to target markets that include surface coatings, food, personal care, pharmaceuticals, oil and gas, plastics and other industrial sectors. Two types of products are available: bulk liquids and liquids in drums. The company carries out four key processes: procurement logistics, external accounting, distribution and sales logistics. Over seven years, the ES journey included the implementation of a number of functionality such as financial, materials management, sales administration and assets management. The system was implemented in four locations, including central warehouse and offices and three regional warehouses.

The Coffee Company

This company is a nationally leading company in Latin America, and it is in the business of processing and distribution of roasted and ground coffee. At the time of the study, the company had been exporting green coffee to the United States and Europe. It earned yearly US$45 million in gross revenues and employed 370 persons. Over seven years, the company implemented an ES in areas such as finance, manufacturing, materials management, sales and distribution, services and transportation. The company also implemented functionality related to executive information and mobile devices. In total, the company implemented this ES in 14 locations, including the factory, the procurement center and 12 regional sales and distribution centers.

The Engineering Company

This company is also located in Latin America. The company's task is the engineering, procurement and construction of large crude oil and energy facilities such as refineries and electrical plants. The company is considered one of the world's 50 most important engineering and procurement companies in the energy sector. The company performs two million man-hours annually through different regional locations to execute projects in the Caribbean, North, Central and South America, the Middle East and Europe. Over five years, the ES journey included the implementation of a number of functional areas such as financial, assets management, materials management, human resources and executive information systems. The study was mainly carried out in the company's headquarters.

The IT Company

At the time of the study, the IT Company was one of the largest hardware and personal computer manufacturers in the world. Now it is a sub-brand of another multinational of more than US$50 billion. The merging process would allow the new company to achieve economies of scale and cost reduction to lower prices and offer better services. The ES journey was studied over two years and then revisited six years later. The study focused on the functionality of financial and assets management. Other functionality was featured in the company but was not considered in the original study. The ES journey included the implementation of the system through 16 offices. The study took place in two locations in the UK.

The Machine Company

The Machine Company is a multinational electronic manufacturing company, originally founded in the United States, but now part of a larger conglomerate. It operates in five continents and specialized in digital appliances and media. At the time of this study, the company's turnover was around US$ 100 billion. The study focused on the Chinese factory, which makes a range of domestic and industrial appliances. The study ran over five years including the implementation of several functionalities, including financial, manufacturing, materials management, distribution and sales, executive information systems, transportation and assets management.

The Telecom Company

This company is one of the most important corporations in the telecom industry, especially in the mobile infrastructure business. This study took place in Spain over six years and included information from the company's Headquarter and Portuguese branches. Spanish subsidiary was the seventh world market for the Telecom Company, with a turnover of Euros 1.5 billion and with 3,000 employees. The ES study focused on Business-to-Business (B2B) procurement, finance and human resources. In particular, we studied the purchase-to-pay process in Spain and its subsequent reorganization as a European shared service. Other functionality was featured in the company but was not considered in the original study.

The road forward

Organizations need to maximize the value of their existing IT assets. We argue that it takes a long time and a lot of learning. In doing so, organizations need new organizational capabilities and social networks. We develop our argument through seven chapters. The first part of the book focuses on the waveforms of an organization and their relationships. In addition, we describe the technology we already have: enterprise systems. The second part explains in detail the processes of the Long Conversation: Osmosis, Growth and Adaptation. Moreover, we describe the way organizations master ES through the Long Conversation approach. The third part identifies the new set of organizational capabilities needed to support the learning and exploration process behind the ES experience and future technological waves. Finally, we summarize our model with a set of practical guidelines related to the implementation process, knowledge and learning management and the roles played by the different actors. Here is a preview of what is to come in the rest of the book.

Chapter 1: The technology wave, organizations and economic reality

The reality is that it takes a long time and a lot of learning to get the best out of your technology.

To put this into the context of the current economic reality, we are in a crisis. Everyone knows that. What's wrong is that lots of people respond by saying we need more new IT, more tools to change our ways. This is actually a dangerous argument. New tools won't save us now. They are for the future. What businesses need now is to make the most of what they already have, of the investments that they have already incurred. This means that they need new organizational practices, new capabilities and new social networks. They need to continue and intensify a long conversation that they began a few years ago.

In a crisis, the first thing you need to know is where you are. Most likely, for most organizations in most sectors, they are already coming down off the back of a wave of technology investments in ES and the like. This sounds like bad news. It is and it isn't. It is certainly challenging, but on the other hand it can lead to innovative and collaborative patterns of behavior that enhance business efficiency. As the pressure on technology investments decreases, productive values can actually increase. That's the key to survival.

Maybe it all comes down to thinking more radically. People get locked into ways of thinking about their firm that can be quite stifling. They think about functions and an organizational chart. They think about a defined and fixed set of partners and customers. They think about hierarchies. At best, all these models constitute a limited palette. It is important to also think about the waveforms of your organization. Most of all think about the wave of technology innovation and then the wave of organizational capabilities that tracks behind it. As one wave descends, the next comes tumbling over the top. The orthodoxy of management won't help you do this. Instead, we lead you to some more radical and innovative thinking, that a lot of people reject. In particular, we focus on the work of economists such as Kondratiev and Schumpeter.

Chapter 2: Enterprise systems: The technology we already have

ES applications include Enterprise Resource Planning (ERP), Customer Relationship Management (CRM), Human Resource Management (HRM),

Product Lifecycle Management (PLM) and Supply Chain Management (SCM). Such systems are widely heralded as a departure in the short history of modern information systems. They enable the integration of business processes within organizations and allow the improvement of coordination among departments, business units and supply chain partners (suppliers and customers). ES are often composed of different functionality and applications provided either by a single vendor or by a set of different vendors (i.e., best-of-breed approach). New information technologies and new means of delivery are making these systems both more affordable and more flexible. For example, new cloud-based offerings cut costs and complexity.

Chapter 3: Biological evolution: osmosis, growth and adaptation

The "Long Conversation" approach comprises three vital elements of learning and development. Each tends to create emergent complexity that can set the implementation back and reorient it away from its original focus and toward group-learning. They are as follows: osmosis, growth and adaptation. Placing these three vital points together is what makes for technology mastery, something that relies on the formal and informal sharing of knowledge about technology and the affected processes and structures.

Chapter 4: Mastery is a long conversation

Far from offering a quick fix, or providing a fast track to an order of magnitude improvement, we argue that ES are better understood through a slow and diligent learning process. They present employees with an opportunity to relearn daily tasks that they had hitherto thought routine, and to forge new bonds and to share new insights in the process. Our empirical studies suggest that it can take up to six years from the adoption of ES to reach the point at which organizations report that they have fully mastered the technology and processes. If this sounds like bad news for those looking for a quick solution to pressing business problems, this chapter offers an alternative understanding of how to master ES. Slow learning processes in pursuit of technical mastery are traditionally common in high-tech businesses, where shared mastery of technology and operational processes is key to the overall success of the enterprise.

Chapter 5: Building organizational capabilities for the long conversation

After the initial phase of ES adoption, results usually do not match initial expectations. However, managers realize that a new mutual cross-understanding between business and IT people has emerged, which can be leveraged to embark in a new promising phase of ES adoption. The new phase should take a long-term perspective and the form of an open discovery, exploration and learning process: it is a Long Conversation.

As managers understand that they are dealing with unstructured complexity, a transition occurs from the initial mechanistic approach to a more organic approach. ES adoption is not a disruption handled via project management to restore normality as soon as possible (mechanistic); it is a transplant handled by socio-technical adaptation (organic). The organic approach requires a new set of organizational capabilities: an involved and developmental leadership style that creates a supporting atmosphere for learning and exploration; a collaborative network of key users engaged in collective action-learning and knowledge diffusion; process and IT specialist functioning under a prototype mindset, and a transition from traditional structured planning and control to management by directed incrementalism.

Chapter 6: Prepare new technology for the next wave

New technology is vital because it drives value, and what matters most is big, platform technology – infrastructural advances. The mistake organizations make is plotting wave after wave of technology advancement without nurturing the value-creating waves in-between. These are where organizational capabilities have been developed, but it will take a long time to extend its growth, osmosis and adaptation. The reality of business is to have long-term perspective whereby you look to the organizational capabilities beyond the next wave of technology. In the meantime, you carry on generating value from what you have and working with tactical, intermediate and cheap technology enhancements.

Chapter 7: Final practical Guidelines

The application of the Long Conversation approach has an important set of implications. We have highlighted a number of critical issues to be considered for the management of the long conversation model. They are related to the implementation process, knowledge and learning management and the roles played by the CEO, the key users and the technology team. We describe them by comparing how these issues are managed in a traditional implementation of IT and how they should be managed when running the long conversation.

OPEN DOOR

So, we invite the readers to join us on a challenging journey to understand what the Long Conversation can do for their organizations. Going step by step will ensure a sustained IT success. We encourage you to apply this learning to your own organization.

OSWALDO LORENZO
Madrid, Spain
PETER KAWALEK
Manchester, UK
GASTÓN GONZÁLEZ
Caracas, Venezuela
BOUMEDIENE RAMDANI
Bristol, UK
February 2011

Acknowledgements

We may have spent many days and nights working over our laptops in pursuit of the completion of this book. We could have not done it without the support, encouragement and advice of many people and organizations.

This book has been drawn from the results of our investigation that has been published in different journals and conferences such as *California Management Review*, *Communications of Association for Information Systems*, *Information and Management*, the European Conference on Information Systems, the Americas Conference on Information Systems and the European Conference in Operations Management. We thank the group of editors and reviewers, who contributed with their feedback and critique to the development and refinement of our ideas and models.

We especially thank the hundreds of people (i.e., CEOs, top executives, managers and employees) who participated in our investigation and provided us with a lot of information and data related to enterprise systems implementation, diffusion and use in their organizations. Our contribution would have been impossible without their time and trust in us.

We would particularly like to thank the IE Business School. In particular, a special 'thank you' goes to Marco Trombetta, Vice Dean of Research at IE Business School and Cynthia Fernandez Lazaro, Director of IE Publishing Department, for encouraging and supporting us to undertake the final effort that led to this book. We are grateful to Gill Hopkins, who helped us many hours in editing activities. We also thank Des Dearlove and Stuart Crainer, who helped us to translate our concepts into more powerful ideas.

We are grateful to Warwick Business School, Manchester Business School and IE Business School for their support and teaching throughout our professional development. Their classrooms, corridors and coffee shops have been the places where many of our ideas and thoughts emerged.

The ideas, constructs and models presented in this book were developed and inspired over a period of many years through a number of stimulating and reflective conversations with a group of colleagues and friends in academic and business environments. In particular, we would like to thank

Colm Butler, Angel Diaz, Paul Esqueda, Mark Greenwood, Ian Kendrick, Michael Margey, Amit Mitra, Yong Ni, Jack O'Herlihy, Bob Snowdon, Brian Warboys, Trevor Wood-Harper, Jeff Word, Densil Williams and Igor Yakimovich.

Joaquin Pérez worked with us particularly in the subject of enterprise system flexibility. He provided us with his knowledge, as an SAP expert, of new enterprise systems trends and capabilities. Yong Ni provided us with information and insights from his research that complement our understanding of the enterprise system phenomenon.

We would also like to recognize the support from Expertia Consulting Group. In particular, we thank Oliver Cardenas, Francisco Perez and Manuel Ruiz, for his support in the development and management of the new blog www.longconversation.com, which functions as our continuous "ideas-room."

Finally, and most importantly, we have to thank our wives, Anna, Ilhem, Marisolina, Yvonne, and children Caitlin, Estefanía, Fabiola, Juan José, Natasha and Rosanna. Without their ongoing support, we would not have fulfilled this achievement. We dedicate this book to them.

Oswaldo Lorenzo is Professor of Management at IE Business School. He specializes in information technology, business process management and supply chain management. His research interests lie in the implementation, assimilation and diffusion of enterprise systems for the purpose of improving processes and supply chains. Professor Lorenzo's extensive experience in this field has led organizations in different sectors (e.g., automobile, banking, government and energy) to contract his consulting services. He has been visiting professor at Manchester Business School (UK), IESA Business School (Venezuela), INCAE (Costa Rica) and Bordeaux School of Management (France). Part of his experience comes from his work on publications for specialized journals such as *California Management Review*, *Journal of Business Ethics*, *Supply Chain Management Review*, *Communications of the Association for Information Systems*, *International Journal of Simulation and Process Modeling*, *Revista de Empresa* and *Revista Latinoamericana de Administración*. He received his PhD from Warwick Business School (UK), his MBA from IESA (Venezuela) and his B.Sc in Industrial Engineering from Carabobo University (Venezuela).

Peter Kawalek is Professor of Information Systems and Strategy at Manchester Business School (UK). He has experience through different roles and contributions in Warwick Business School (UK), IE Business School (Spain) and Letterkenny Institute of Technology. Professionally, Professor Kawalek has worked on board level with companies, on short projects with government ministers and at all sorts of levels with public-sector agencies. These organizations include O2, Office of the Taoiseach, SAP, Chubb Insurance Company of Europe, BT, GNER, Journey 9, United Utilities, Hoverspeed, Fujitsu, Jaguar Cars, Department of Communities and Local Government, Cabinet Office, Salford City Council, Oldham Council, Leeds City Council and the NHS.

Gastón González is a Director of Expertia Consulting Group, a multinational management consulting firm. For more than two decades, he has been a professor of Strategy, Organization and Information Technology at IESA Business School and Universidad Simón Bolívar at Caracas,

Venezuela. He has an extensive 25 year experience as a business and management consultant for board level and C-level, in different countries, in topics such as business strategy, corporate governance, mergers and acquisitions and business model innovation. Mr. González has been part of successful business cases of leading companies in financial services, media, consumer goods, food & beverage and technology, among others. He holds an MBA focused in Strategy and Corporate Finance from the University of Miami, an M.Sc.E in Computer, Information and Control Engineering from the University of Michigan. He is also an Electronic Engineer from Universidad Simón Bolívar at Caracas-Venezuela.

Boumediene Ramdani is Senior Lecturer in Strategy and Operations Management at Bristol Business School, UK. His research interests lie in IT-enabled business change, particularly in the role required of senior managers to successfully orchestrate such change. His research investigates how senior managers can most effectively select, implement and deploy IT to achieve business goals. He has worked with a number of private and public sector organizations such as CA Technologies, Datamonitor.com and UK Department of Communities & Local Government. His current consulting activity focuses on advising firms on strategy-related matters and how to unlock business value from their IT investments.

ABBREVIATIONS

APICS	American Production and Inventory Control Society
B2B	Business to Business
BI	Business Intelligence
BPR	Business Process Redesign
CAPEX	Capital Expenditures
CPFR	Collaborative Planning Forecasting and Replenishment
CRM	Customer Relationship Management
DRP	Distribution Resource Planning
EAI	Enterprise Application Integration
ERP	Enterprise Resource Planning
ES	Enterprise System
HRM	Human Resource Management
IS	Information System
IT	Information Technology
KPI	Key Performance Indicators
KUC	Key User Committee
MRO	Maintenance, Repairs and Operations
MRP	Manufacturing Resource Planning
NPV	Net Present Value
PLM	Product Lifecycle Management
RFM	Requisition for Material
SCM	Supply Chain Management
SLT	Social Learning Theory
STS	Socio-Technical System Theory
XPM	Extreme Project Management

CHAPTER 1

The technology wave, organizations and economic reality

A long conversation

It takes a long time and a lot of hard work for your business to master its information technology (IT). It is an ongoing challenge. Even if it ever does so, if all workers feel they are able to use all the features that they need without difficulty, the effect might be transient or even an illusion. In the modern technological environment, the latent potential of IT can often go untapped, and any given set of practices can be subject to challenge from new business requirements.

Implementation projects will be closed at some point, and it will be declared that the firm has achieved the objectives of its initial business case, but the bigger story is that they enter a new reality. In this new reality, learning must continue and new practices must be developed. Only then do organizations reach the full potential of the system and then, after that, innovate beyond it.

Let's apply a little context to these statements and then develop them further. Implicit in this sketch is a large- or medium-sized firm operating with some sophisticated combination of IT systems. Probably, there is some sort of Enterprise System (ES) operating as a platform. Around it will be some other applications, some of which will be fully integrated with the platform, some partially integrated and some stand-alone. Beyond these will be the profusion of applications at the desktop, on smart phones and on phones. Through all these systems, the operational and managerial activities of the business are conducted.

Now, it is not only obvious but important to note that to master any given part of this technology requires significant investment of effort. The main platform systems will be especially complex and present a particular challenge. They are absolutely crucial to the business as they interact with individuals, teams, partners and customers. Groups of people have to learn about the functionality of the systems, and every individual can be affected by everybody else's performance. Call it a kind of organizational choreography machine, if you will. Now, add in the observation that beyond the workable functionality of IT at any given point in time is likely to lie some latent potential. Most likely, as our case studies report, the organization has settled for a level of competency that is sufficient but probably not optimal and not maximal.

What all of this amount to is that we need to enlarge our view of what IT is and how we manage it through projects? We will show that IT projects are usually a kind of accounting convenience that relate to only a part of a much greater IT journey. Somewhere it is declared that the business case has been satisfied. But the drive for learning and development continues. Moreover, the logic continues and organizations see that the value of these IT systems lies in complex patterns of their use, well beyond the remit of IT projects and well beyond their initial expectations. It is vital to understand and optimize how teams learn about IT long after the official project team has closed its office and gone away. All of this has implications for the economics of the technology and how we should think about that. Using standard concepts and new case insights, we will explore how large-scale IT adoption can be better structured and understood.

Longtime and even lifetime journeys with IT, rather than the shorter "IT project": this is our Long Conversation. The idea conjures up the ongoing ebb and flow of learning is essential to value creation and efficiency. This learning eventually extends and becomes a source of innovation.

At the beach

We had two conversations on the beach. The first was in Torrox, near the city of Malaga in Spain. There the waves rise steeply in a swell before cascading down to make the shore. When we were there, the sun was bright and the sky blue. It was a typical, hot Spanish summer morning. The beach was quickly filled with families, couples and friends and soon every parasol was taken.

The weather was also beautiful, albeit less typically, when we assembled at Rossnowlagh Beach in County Donegal, Ireland. This is a quiet, expansive beach. We visited in the spring of the year following our conversation in Torrox. At Rossnowlagh, the waves are different, rolling in gently over a long distance and swirling over a break. It is popular with surfers, and we took our children out for some practice on a board.

Later, from the Smuggler's Inn that stands on the cliffs above the beach, we settled down to have some lunch. From our high vantage point, we watched the waves and their shapes. As each wave ran out to make the shore, the energy within was the energy expended. Of course, if we tell you that our conversations were about technology and business, maybe you will be surprised. Normally, beaches are places where people go to talk about their lives and the movement of their dreams. They don't normally sit there talking about work and technology. Never mind, maybe it was because we had spent more than a decade studying the movement of ES technology through organizations that we thought it would be a good idea to relocate ourselves to the beach. It gave us a chance to think about our work and what it means to all the people around us.

One thing that always concerned us was that business today seems like an endless fashion parade. It is an almost perpetual strut of new ideas and technologies through the workplace. Many of these seem to promise the Earth. But do they deliver? All carry an implicit threat: if you don't know about this and someone else does, you will be at a painful disadvantage. As technology professionals and enthusiasts, we could understand this. Some commentators argue that we are living in exponential times. Indeed, probably, we agree. There are new technology announcements every day. This is exciting. But how should one cope with that? How many of them matter? How many new technologies matter to you? And, anyway, how do you best cope with fast and vigorous change? Do you jump to it project by project just as some kind of hyperactive frog? Do you buy more and more technical expertise? Do you downgrade your business experts and promote your techies? Or do you do something sensible? Does the challenge prompt you to look evermore deeply at your organization and to understand the processes by which it learns and adapts?

We were concerned because our studies were showing us a different reality to that we read about in books. In reality, we were finding that businesses assimilated technology slowly, certainly much more slowly than they intended. We also found that they tended to derive great value from the journey of learning about technology, or that they at least did so to the degree in which they involved staff in the learning process. We were finding that technology adoption was a slow, communal process.

We were studying enterprise systems. This is important. Enterprise systems are the backbone of modern business – large, multi-functional, IT. It is not easy to adopt such systems. Nonetheless, we could see that there were certain key principles emerging. These principles were consistent with ideas of disruption, or radical change to technological platforms, and the difficult processes of diffusion that followed thereon.

Back under the parasols at Torrox, we looked out at the horizon and discussed the big picture. History teaches us that society moves uncomfortably over different technology platforms. When something big happens – let's take the invention of the printing press as an example – there are winners and losers. There is conflict. Some people embrace the new. Some have reason to fear it. Some oppose it utterly. New technology seems to be accompanied by a great shock and then a long echo of assimilation, learning and change. Johannes Gutenberg's invention of the printing press seems a good illustration of these generalities at this macro, societal level.

Could it be the same at the organizational level, at the level of a single business? Is there a kind of pattern wherein a new technology platform comes into the business as a kind of a shock or challenge, but then stimulates a longer process of adaptation and learning? We sketched the model as a kind of waveform, and we talked about the economic theories of Nikolai Kondratieff and Joseph Schumpeter. Were we playing with the same kind of phenomena, albeit on a different scale? Could the single organization experience the calamity and potential of disruption, and then the long but valuable wash of the wave?

Technology investments and the knowledge to harness them

When an organization adopts a substantial new IT system, it goes through an upsurge of effort and learning. This effort, which again we describe as a kind of shock, peaks at some point, turning into a longer process of infusion, nurturing and innovation (Figure 1.1).

Very sensibly, what project management of IT implementation tries to do is to use methods and organizational principles to flatten the height of the curve. With proper project management, goes the argument, the effort of adoption should not be so great. Moreover, your business will quickly return to normal.

It follows that the conventional proposition of project management is to create an alternative curve, one that appears to be more manageable to the business. We could sketch this project management proposition in many ways, but a defensible version is given in Figure 1.2.

What we see depicted is something that requires great effort and then, at some point coinciding with the termination of the project, lessens and returns to something "normal." The project was but a brief, managed interruption to the normal life of the business. Now, three corrections need to be added to amend the proposition. These are based on our long-term, empirical studies. The first is that the effort required in the project always exceeds that which was anticipated. The curve is steeper, and the peak is

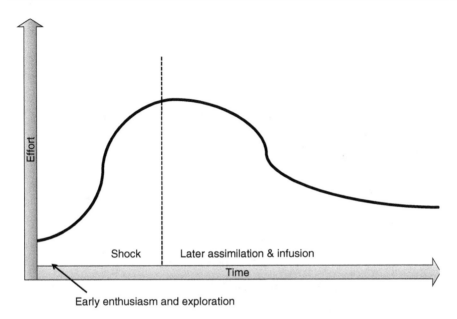

Figure 1.1 Template of major systems adoption

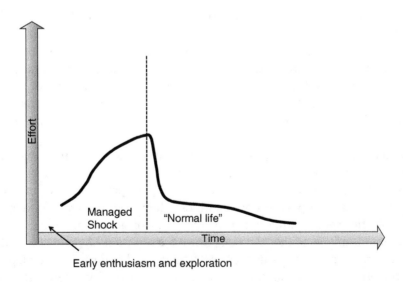

Figure 1.2 The project management proposition

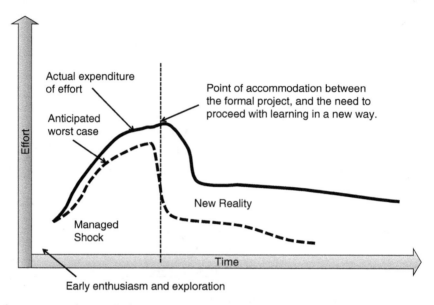

Figure 1.3 What really happens

higher. The second correction is that the ending of the project does not coincide with a lessening of effort and a return to normal business life. Instead, there is a negotiated accommodation over the end of the project. This is not actually the point at which the major effort is done, but rather marks a reorientation of the effort so it is based more on internal effort through organizational initiatives. Finally, what businesses then discover is that there is great value in the extended period of learning and adjustment that follows the ending of the official project. "Normal life" never returns and efforts to diffuse the IT continue, as do efforts to learn about its capabilities. The upside of this, though, is that businesses report great value in these post-project activities.

Remember, we are talking about ES – large scale IT – the great platform systems of our empirical studies. Moreover, note that the figures are only sketches. We are depicting the dynamics of process rather than trying to articulate proportions or quantities. Then from within these dynamics, note the special importance of the point of accommodation. As we have noted, this is neither the peak nor the expiration of effort. Instead, it marks a reorientation towards self-sufficiency and control from within the organization. This marks the transition to a new reality where the effort to assimilate and maximize the potential of the new technology remains higher than was originally anticipated. This fact may be bad news, but our evidence is that the benefits of this new reality are also greater than expectations. As the effort to master new systems continues, so too advantages of team learning and shared knowledge are unexpectedly uncovered. The large-scale IT system has catalyzed a whole organizational movement.

When we talk of the Long Conversation, we are talking of the whole process of living with IT, from its conception, past the point of accommodation and through into the ongoing processes of learning. In particular, the latter stages intrigue, for there is no return to an imagined normality. Rather, processes of infusion and diffusion take hold; these germinated from earlier decisions in the project phase of the implementation. We see it as akin to a biological process, sometimes comparing it to a body receiving an organ transplant, and we utilize the terms "growth," "osmosis" and "adaptation." The conversation, all the talking and learning, all the workshops, the designations of roles, the committees, and the exemplary behavior of a few key users, become the means by which change is accomplished. It is a conversation, a long conversation, with many turns and moments and stresses. It becomes a wave, a sonic wave perhaps, but composed of thousands and thousands of social interactions. Looking at IT systems in this way helps us understand how value is really created. The process of social change is not only where the effort is but also where the value is.

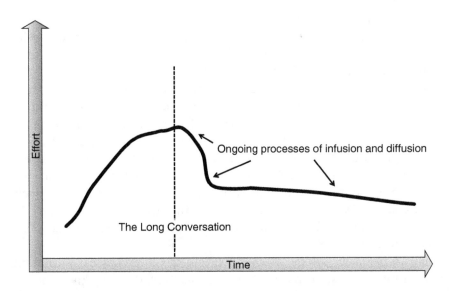

Figure 1.4 The long conversation

Mental models

We have been to the blue-chip boardroom and we have been to the factory floor, and we have met talented people in both positions. One thing we have observed is that how you think about your business organization is really important. People who do well, people who cope with change well, seem to think about the organization in a particular way. It is not that they somehow have some arbitrarily different set of ideas; it is that the very processes of their thinking are different. Let us dwell on this a little before returning to the main ideas of the Long Conversation and the waveforms of business.

These days, whatever your brand or logo says, the dominant image that most workers in your organization carry around in their heads is the organizational chart. If they were asked to draw a picture of the business, most likely, this is what they would draw. There would be the CEO and the board at the top and then all the spikes and lines of the divisional heads and their subordinates. By drawing an organization in this way, the workers would be depicting it as a power structure that is something like an army. It is also something like a pitchfork, which in some ways is an interesting allusion. Our point, though, is that this typical organizational chart is just one way of depicting an organization. It has some merits but also conceals much, and you would not want to put too much faith in it. It is not a complete explanation of how an organization works, nor, even, of how power is managed within it.

Argyris[1] utilizes the term "mental model." It is a useful term that helps us understand how we think. It originates in psychology, having its roots in the work of Kenneth Craik.[2] In management, as well as Argyris, other writers such as Pierre Wack[3] and Peter Senge[4] have explored the implications of the concept. Basically, the idea is that we always operate with some abstraction of reality. We never know the full detail of what is going on. Instead we have some kind of model of reality that is built up over time and largely through experience. The important point, though, is that it is not reality: it is just a model. Even in our most familiar environments just as our domestic lives, we operate through a model of what is, or is likely to be, going on. We do not really know the full detail, complexity and the entire set of motivations and aspirations. We settle for an abstraction, a model, instead.

This is what we allude to when we talk of the processes of thinking being different for some people. Some people think that they know the full story (i.e. they don't think they work through a model) and consequently get into a state of lockdown, or resistance, when change happens. Other people know that they do not know the whole story. They constantly seek to test, replenish, revise or replace the models that they possess. We believe that this latter group of thinkers is better in circumstances of learning and change.

From a business point of view, it is important to be alive to the fact that the whole thing operates through a great series of models; the interplay of everybody's partial understanding of the business. Management is concerned with the cultivation and feeding of models. Managers want all stakeholders, including themselves, to develop models that lead to beneficial outcomes for them and the business as a whole. Considering this, we can return to the example of the organization chart. If you think that it is the only legitimate model of the organization, then you will trim your behavior to a series of permissions and rules that is based on that view. Yet, the chart is only a partial representation of power structures. It is certainly not a useful model of organizational learning or the journey that a business makes with a particular technology. It does not describe dynamics, process, culture or the tacit.

So, with this we argue that effective change relies on being able to think about it properly and the key recognition that we are all, always, working with a partial understanding of what is going on. It follows from this that equipping ourselves with good models that we can think about and then develop is important.

Let us illustrate this by returning to the new economic "reality," and the pressure that is upon business because of the market failures that gripped nations before, during and after our visits to Torrox (2009) and Rossnowlagh (2010). This economic calamity happened because powerful people in society believed in a series of models that turned out to be ill-tuned and false. They believed that financial markets were in and of themselves a source of wealth; they believed that expert and self-interested stakeholders would be good guardians of a system that privileged them; they believed that new sources of economic wealth could be found in developed societies through the manipulation of consumer systems and loans – as though they were extracting more coal from a seam.

Perhaps more than anything, they made the mistake of believing in certainty itself. People thought they knew the full story and indeed they had evidence that each of their models might be true. The mistake was perhaps in believing that this kind of truth was possible, when they never had more than a model.

Therefore, what this means is that the models presented in this book are, well, models. They are useful abstractions that help to explain the journey made as an organization seeks to build value through technology. Let's

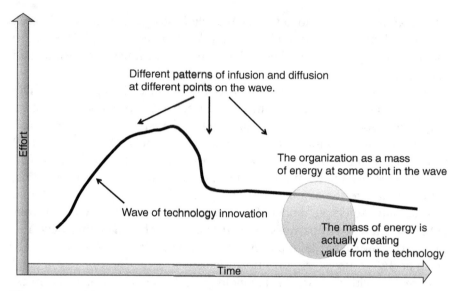

Figure 1.5 The organization's journey on a wave of innovation

take Figure 1.4 as one example. It is our sketch (remember, only a sketch) of the dynamics of the Long Conversation. It gives a new way of thinking about your organization. Start with a major technology platform in your mind. This might well be your ES. Ask yourself where the organization is along the wave of this system. Is it near the beginning, the middle or the end? Wherever it is, there will be different dynamics of learning and social interaction. Think about your organization as a school within, and then a fusion of activity around, this wave. Thinking in this way gives you a new way of thinking about it. It is a bit different to the traditional organizational chart. Where does it sit on a wave of innovation? At any given point of time, the journey will have different characteristics that need to be managed.

Waves of technology innovation

At a macro-economic level, Schumpeter's ideas of creative destruction tell of how society moves over the plates of great technological shift.[5] Intense effort and conflict precedes a much longer process of enhancement and refinement. At some point, this longer process is itself interrupted by the sudden emergence of a new technology platform. This is creative destruction. A great swell of effort accompanies the destruction, as a new technology is implanted into society, bringing creativity.

Schumpeter was an Austrian. He was born in 1883, roughly a century after Eric Hobsbawn claimed industrial revolution "broke out" in Great Britain, but only 36 years after the birth of Thomas Edison. Dying in the United States in January 1950, a month before he would have reached the age of 67, Schumpeter lived to see huge shifts in the technological platforms of society. He also saw the horrendous conflicts of World War I and World War II; each conflict won by the forces able to muster a technological advantage over its enemies. Originally a lawyer, but famous as an economist and political scientist, Schumpeter is also a kind of forensic historian. His works help us interpret the age we are living through, and that which we are headed into. Remember, some theorists talk of our times now as "exponential."[6]

Schumpeter remains a very interesting figure. According to published recollections, he struggled for recognition of his ideas and was not known as being a good teacher by his students at Harvard. Nonetheless, the simple almost poetic idea of the crash of new technology through society, and the burning off of old ideas, like waste, or swailing fields, seems to resonate. It seems to signify our age. Deeper inside Schumpeter's writing are more elaborate ideas. His model contained waves within waves, the great crash and rise of technologies enfolding smaller cycles of informational, infrastructural and demographic waves. Moreover, he took an absolute position, opposing the prevailing orthodoxy of Keynesianism, and deriding its fiscal management approaches as "interference."

Behind the work of Schumpeter stands that of the Russian, Kondratieff.[7] Nine years younger than Schumpeter, Kondratieff would die sooner, executed by the forces of Josef Stalin for whom he had worked as an economics advisor. Kondratieff's insight was that capitalist economies travelled through great waves of 50 and 60 years before reaching calamity. According to Kondratieff, after calamity came renewal, and it was this claim, that capitalism does not face inevitable decline but regenerates that dissatisfied his Stalinist commanders. Kondratieff's observations, though, were again based on observations of technological innovation driving investment and change.

With Kondratieff's technological waves as his base, Schumpeter developed a model, combining the economic cycles from the work of Kuznets (demographic cycles), Juglar[8] (investment cycles) and Kitchin[9] (information lags). Each of these waves of economic activity has a different time span, with Kondratieff the longest at 50/60 years, Kuznets moving over 15 and more years, Juglar at up to 11 years and Kitchin cycling over 3 to 5 years. This complete model arguably accounts for the movement of technology in society and provides a complete impression of the dynamics of economies.

These ideas of great technological eras driving the innovation and modernization of business are, at once, interesting. The business becomes something that is founded on the capabilities of a new technology or else something that is already founded, but which grasps at the new and seeks to devour its capabilities. Business is always placed somewhere on a technology wave. It has no other normality.

Hence, we draw parallels between what we see in global technology waves and how a single business or organization then behaves. Inside the great economic wave are thousands of businesses and organization all mimicking each other, all shoving in the same direction. In some ways, this is an obvious point. It is just a movement of scale, from the macro-economics of Kondratieff and Schumpeter to the organizational reification of these ideas in individual enterprises. However, we also cautiously extend it to make it an analogy, and to see the internal behavior of enterprises as taking the multi-wave shape of society as a whole. Businesses are not static structures. They are not pitchforks. They are communities. These communities move with and in relation to technology.

Inside our Long Conversation are waves and cycles of infusion and diffusion. We repeat that we see patterns of osmosis, growth and adaptation. These constitute the diffusion of capabilities throughout the organization

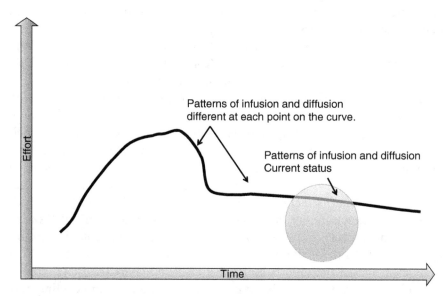

Figure 1.6 Patterns of infusion and diffusion

(the osmosis factor), the mastery of more sophisticated uses of technological capability (growth) and changes to the business model (the adaptation factor). Then, beyond these lies a greater, collective wave and beyond this, a greater technology wave. It is by studying these and seeing them in action and interaction that we understand how a single organization moves with its technology. In the end, it is all to do with social processes. Organizations have to push out and share technology among their membership (and new versions of that technology) and also to elevate understanding of that technology.

Platforms for the organization: enterprise systems

Let's talk a little more specifically about IT. We feel it is important to think about platforms; fundamental, large scale systems that provide a backbone for the organization. There are many different kinds of system that are important to us, but we need to start with these platforms. Talk of "platforms" to IT managers in modern, and mostly they will assume that you are talking of a special class of systems called Enterprise Systems (ES) or, a little more traditionally, Enterprise Resource Planning (ERP). For the last 20 years, companies have been implementing and adopting these ES. They have done this for many purposes. Logically, they will talk of needing to automate transactions, reduce costs, increase customer satisfaction, integrate with suppliers, and make better decisions. Sometimes, they will also admit to great competitive pressures, the need to build integrative networks and the fear of being left out.

Examples of ES include applications for ERP, Customer Relationship Management (CRM), Human Resource Management (HRM), Product Lifecycle Management (PLM) and Supply Chain Management (SCM). Such systems have been often heralded as a significant step in the short history of modern information systems (IS). In the jargon of business, they enable the integration of business processes within organizations and allow the improvement of coordination among departments, business units and supply chain partners (suppliers and customers). Trying to express this to the layman, we might talk of big and complex IT systems that allow at least a base level of automation through the enterprise and sometimes, very sophisticated functionality indeed.

ES are typically composed of different functionality and applications provided by either a single vendor or a set of different vendors. This latter approach is known as a best-of-breed approach. Also notable is that ES are typically standard, at least in part. Different organizations, even competitive businesses, adopt similar systems. Customizations can be different, but fundamentally the drive is towards a common platform.

If all of this begins to sound complex, then good. It is right that it seems so. ES can be hugely complex. It is important to acknowledge this and to see the challenge that this entails for the adopting organization. As we will argue later, ultimately, the purchase of an ES is the purchase of the future. Whether this is an open, innovative future or something restrictive and frustrating is down, at least in part, to how successfully the organization masters the ES. Note again the term "infusion" here. Higher levels of infusion mean that the business has more effectively mastered the technology.

Yet, as you know already, infusion is only half of the story. The other part of the conversation is about diffusion. ES are multi-functional and integrative. Companies often implement the system using a phased scheme in such a way that each phase forms part of an entire journey. The term here is "diffusion," of course.

Finally, note that even in the simplest of rollouts, the adoption of ES in one business area may necessitate changes to the system already operational in related areas. Likewise, as an area of functionality becomes utilized, adaptations and enhancements may be applied. For environmental reasons, or just because staff have got to know the system better, changes may be made. This raises the question of when implementation actually ends. In fact, it never ends. You have read this argument already, but it is not just this set of authors who says this. We were intrigued to pick up a report on the web. It concerned a discussion panel in the conference.[10] There, experts talked about the completion of ES deployment, concluding that many of these projects are simply never completed in any conventional sense. Normality never returns.

Perhaps what this should give us is an enlarged sense of what a project is, or what it purports to affect. With this come some challenges. A normal way of building a business case for IT investment is through a calculation of "Net Present Value" (NPV). This is basically a way of counting the sum of cash flows over a fixed time series and can be used for capital projects of many kinds. Fundamentally, the "long" aspect of seeing the Long Conversation is problematic for NPV calculations. The further in time the intangible benefits materialize, the more heavily they are discounted in NPV and the less their economic value is seen to be. This requires some enlargement of thinking and a preparedness to reject the basic notion that an IT project is "done" and then, somehow, the organization returns to "normal." It is important to understand that the organization is changed forever, and there are opportunities for value way beyond the horizon of the conventional IT project. This is often realized indirectly. For example,

Organizational Development and its training projects are not logically separable from the technology platform and often relate directly to it. Thus, by many means, and often long after it has ceased to pursue an IT project, an organization will pursue initiatives that deepen infusion or broaden diffusion. These initiatives might be called "team development," "training" or "quality excellence," but they are all part of the new normality and contribute to ongoing learning.

Moreover, there are two cases that help unpick the value of thinking through the Long Conversation in the context of IT investments.

- You manage a firm that has already spent some years in an ES project. You have recently closed the project or are about to close it. All previous investments are sunk costs, and most likely benefits have been much less than expected and costs are much higher. This situation is not uncommon. The opportunity is for the business case to start afresh with the "soft," post-project part of the Long Conversation. Its otherwise intangible benefits are not far away in the future. This is a key part of the motivation behind the Long Conversation and has particular relevance to executives seeking to maximize the value of their assets. An important message of the book is that it is easy and common to leave the potential of ES partially untapped. Many organizations struggle to achieve infusion and even diffusion. In the economic crisis of today, this is even more markedly wasteful. There is argument to be made that executives should milk the current IT platform. We would argue that many enterprises have potential for new post-implementation projects that contribute to an overall Long Conversation.
- Your firm has not yet started the great pursuit of ES, and you are reading about the reality of the experience in this book. So, you start doubting your business case, knowing that tangible benefits will probably be less than expected; capital expenditure (CAPEX) will be larger and intangible benefits more likely to develop over time. You feel tempted to discard the project. What advice can be advanced? Well, it has to be acknowledged that many large IT investments do not have a positive outcome. Thinking about the Long Conversation alerts you to inflated medium-term project-based business cases. It helps you to refine your approach to both the leading and trailing edge of the technology wave as it passes through your business. Indeed, case studies from many sources suggest that many firms jump onto a bandwagon without even knowing where it is headed. They implement large IT applications because it is fashionable, maybe because their competitors did it, or because a large customer asked them. It is important to be realistic about large-scale IT. It is not easy.

A full, useful business case can be built and structured incrementally as a set of scenarios. These should compare the cash flow of the investment against the cash flow of doing nothing and trying to maintain the current situation. This current situation is, of course, dynamic, and it might be subject to negative pressures. Competitor pressures and their movements in the IT market will affect it, as will other market conditions. Thus, one scenario might be very negative: facing more technologically advanced competitors, your company's growth might stagnate and your margins might get crunched. An incremental business case of this sort is less concerned with seeking the advantages of IT, but rather seeks to avoid the disadvantages of not making the investment. The IT investment might be described as "a necessary evil."

Moreover, in the technology-focused early stages of the project-based, the Long Conversation advises against over-investment. Managers should beware of trusting in a short-term materialization of tangible benefits. An alternative to the typical big-bang implementation is to phase implementation. Later, we will exemplify these processes of osmosis, adaptation and growth. Understanding these, the enterprise may envision adoption as a series of mini-waves. At the beginning, the movement should focus on areas of the business where there are low-maturity levels and opportunities for growth are greatest. The adoption process should be seeking to focus on business areas where the best opportunities exist for creating value through automation and/or coordination. This initial mini-wave has the potential to pay for itself and be NPV positive. Before it ends, a new mini-wave (again, enacted through osmosis, adaptation and growth) will identify new areas of the business, where incremental benefits are attractive enough to surpass incremental costs and hence be NPV positive.

If previous mini-waves have been NPV positive, each succeeding one will have to justify itself with a lower burden of new investment. Then, as several successful mini-waves unfold, the technology focus of the project dissipates and a new focus on social learning becomes obvious and central. Understanding the Long Conversation is herein a way of proceeding with low incremental investments that leverages learning to promote intangible benefits growth.

Marshalling the business case

As this debate turns over, we open up the wider subject of the place and role of a good business case. We have seen them done well and we have seen them done badly, and we are not sure that the abilities of managers always determine which is which. Rather, we point to the additional influence of the business environment and the dynamics that affect business plans and proposals.

In short, the business case summarizes the targets that the firm will achieve at different points in time. It becomes the focus of all the NPV calculations and the frequent focus of debate before, during and even after the major implementation project. Can we achieve the business case? Are we on track to achieve the business case? Have we achieved the business case? Perhaps controversially we suggest that eventually the question becomes, *when can we set aside this business case and get on with learning what this system can really do?*

We report that it can take a long time, maybe six years, to achieve the full benefits of an ES. Don't worry. This is not the same as six years to achieve the business case. Rather, the business case is an approximation that may or may not be achieved in full but which will be, necessarily, discarded before osmosis, adaptation and growth reach any kind of zenith. The full benefits of an ES require profound business transformation that creates business value of many sorts; not surprisingly it takes time.

What this means is:

- A financial business case is always incremental or differential: invest in ES versus doing nothing. For companies plagued with the inefficiencies of legacy systems, there are streams of negative cash flow issues (costs associated to the inefficiencies) that are spent before ES adoption. If the company does nothing, there remains the possibility of reduced value to stakeholders and, as a consequence, reduced growth rate and margin compression. Thus, an incremental business case (ES adoption minus current situation) can produce a lot of positive cash flow by eliminating legacy system inefficiencies and not incurring in the "pain" of being left behind in top-line growth and margin health, when compared with industry peers. These are differential cash flows. It means that, even when full business benefits have not been achieved yet, the business case may be comfortably positive. Notice that full business benefits may or may not create competitive advantage; that depends on superior execution versus. Competitors. This is related to Porter's criticism of competitive advantage that is not based on structural strategic choices.[11] He argues that what you are getting is operational excellence, which is good, but typically a non-sustainable advantage. But anyway, through our lens, even if the company does not attain a competitive advantage, the fact that it is not being left behind (i.e. incurring in competitive *disadvantage*) may be more than enough to provide NPV positive interventions.

- The enlarged focus of the Long Conversation is also an incremental process. It might be termed "directed incrementalism" to contrast it with disjointed incrementalism, what Lindblom[12] poetically conjured as "the science of muddling through." This incrementalism is "directed," because it is related to a vision of where it is headed. It is incremental because this is the way learning works out in practice and how the massive uncertainty is handled and then reduced in accumulative cycles. Now, with the Long Conversation lens, we see that after the main implementation project, progress continues through incremental advances in functionality (osmosis, growth and adaptation). These incremental waves can be interpreted as mini-projects (or mini-waves) of differing levels of formality. We see that the big wave of early project activity is eventually followed by smaller but more frequent waves. Beguilingly, and vitally for the hard-headed activities of the firm, it is possible to model all these mini-waves and all are potentially NPV positive. Of course, at a certain point the conversation is exhausted, and ES *business value potential* is no longer positive. Perhaps, we have to wait for a new cycle of Schumpeterian technology innovation.

In this process, we see how the Long Conversation creates economic value while also diminishing organizational and technological risk.

Conclusion

Projects are transitions between realities. Sometimes these realities are very dissimilar, sometimes little changes. To focus on IT projects is restrictive. IT is much more important than that.

It is better to understand the firm as a society, like any other society, that is intimately interwoven with its technology, and which is partially defined by that technology. A key role of managers is to understand where the business is with the technology and how it is progressing. There will be a constant process of learning and adjustment. Making the business effective, and sharp, and profitable, and meaningful, requires this discipline.

We emphasize the importance of ES. This is because they are so significant in scope and complexity that we can call them platforms. They are the long wave of organizational technology. Adopting a new spreadsheet or an appended application will not be so significant, obviously, although it will constitute a part of the same set of forces and learning.

Philosophically, in making these points, we adopt a position that says everyone is working with a partial and partially subjective understanding of the world. Everybody has a mental model. Managerial initiative, methodologies, theories, diagrams and schema are all ways of provoking and changing these models. The diagrams and ideas we have presented here are models; ways of thinking about the organization and the reality of life in business.

Our emphasis on the Long Conversation is designed to move thinking outwards, for the camera to pan across the landscape, and to encourage managers to think about the bigger picture of change. Within this, as we will see in later chapters, there are some particular and detailed processes. These are important because they show how migration with technology is made. We call these Infusion and Diffusion. Infusion and Diffusion are social processes. We are talking about a conversation, of course. As well as encouraging managers to pan across the landscape, we also encourage them to then refocus on particular mechanisms of learning and exchange. The journey with technology is not made by the plan, we suggest, as much as it is made by attention to learning events, knowledge exchange, customs and practices among key users. Good organizations realize this.

When we pack all of this up, and then write it down as a set of ideas and models, we realize that something else is important too. This is that it helps us understand and rethink what we need of IT itself. To be precise, business cannot passively adjust to IT. Nor can it express all its needs through formal requirements. Rather, the Long Conversation reverberates more roundly and has messages for everyone. Remember, all of this is founded upon empirical work; hard-won lessons. One of the key lessons is that IT itself must change. We need systems that support ongoing change and flexibility. We need to explore the relationship of business models, processes and practices, and how technology underpins them. The IT systems of the future must be built with the very basic design principle that they will be deployed as part of a process of evolution and innovation.

CHAPTER 2

Enterprise systems: The technology we already have

Understanding enterprise systems

For the last 20 years, companies have been implementing and adopting large-scale IT, most notably enterprise systems (ES). They have done this to automate transactions, reduce costs, increase customer satisfaction, integrate with suppliers and make better decisions. Examples of ES include applications for Enterprise Resource Planning (ERP), Customer Relationship Management (CRM), Human Resource Management (HRM), Product Lifecycle Management (PLM) and Supply Chain Management (SCM). Such systems are widely heralded as a departure in the short history of modern information technology. They enable the integration of business processes within organizations and allow the improvement of coordination among departments, business units and supply chain partners (suppliers and customers). ES are often composed of different functionality and applications provided either by a single vendor or by a set of different vendors (i.e., what is known as the "best-of-breed" approach).[1]

The dependency of modern business on ES systems is very substantial. It is reported that every Fortune 500 company has an ES.[2] They can be described as the unseen platforms of modern living, enabling consumption and trade across business networks and across the globe. From our shopping trips to internet travel bookings, visits to the pharmacist, or collecting our salaries; lives are lived in constant interaction with ES. Orders, supply, payment, inventory; these are the fodder of ES; they are the transactions and processes that these systems support.

Many authors have reported that ES are complex technologies because of their sheer scale, the off-the-shelf approach to their adoption, and the organizational, operational and technological changes they introduce within organizations.[3] This complexity has made ES implementation an increasingly appealing topic for research among scholars. Reportedly high rates of failure in ES projects resulted in a tendency to analyze this phenomenon from different management perspectives.[4] This means that we can now argue that ES has become a cross-functional discipline in its own right, holding interest for scholars in a broad range of management fields, including IS, organization theory, human resources, accounting and operations.

Meanwhile, the situation evolves and changes year by year. New information technologies and new means of delivery are making these systems both more affordable and more flexible. For example, new cloud-based offerings potentially cut costs and complexity. It is possible to conceive of constantly accessible, customizable "processes in the sky." In the future, maybe, it won't be that ES are complex, implemented products but that they offer accessible interfaces to a myriad of business networks and functionality. ES will be a service, and access to this service will change the costs and convenience of business; from the smallest start-up to the grandest conglomerate.

A step back in time: bureaucracy

The clue is in the name, "bureaucracy." This was for a time and a technology. The technology, principally, was the bureau – a desk. The old image is of workers sat at desks with forms and pens, working in a structured way with heavily structured hierarchy. Take out the bureau, the pen and the form and introduce the application, the device and the network, and things should change, yes? Well, maybe, and maybe not.

Implicit in bureaucracy is the understanding of work being broken up by tasks and into hierarchy. A series of permissions govern what each individual worker can or cannot do. These permissions might be encoded into the form itself and thereby enforced, for example, the worker must tick these boxes and provide these signatures. Beyond this lies a deeper model. This is the idea of the firm itself being a great arrangement of people in tasks and roles, each person striving to fulfill some duty in hope of reward or promotion. Remember what we said about the power of mental models and the pitchfork view of the enterprise, well, we are coming back to that point.

The charge has been made that ES become a kind of "electronic bureaucracy" – heinous control systems, constantly falling out of step with a dynamic business environment or, worse, functioning as an instrument of control by misguided managers. They are like the old bureaucracies but, in a way, worse. At least with pens and forms, everybody understood the technology. Everybody knew the language and could make suggestions about the redesign of a form or, perhaps, how an office processed its operations. In the new age of ES, so the charge goes, the common language is lost and skilled teams become dependent on experts who reside in the IT office or some external consultancy. Control is diminished or lost entirely.

Indeed, there is a good point made in this charge. Our empirical evidence can in some ways be interpreted as a struggle for control, as a contest to find an optimal position between control by users and control by a separate group of experts. As the Long Conversation unfolds, always, there is some reclaiming of control by users and the organization of groups and routines to make this effective.

ES is a constantly evolving technology and we want to use this fact to step over some questions of the coding of processes and how easy they are to change. Instead, we assert as a rough generalization that the trend is toward systems that are more easily controllable and more flexible. We cite some language developments, graphical programming, common interfaces and some of the work on cloud-based systems as evidence in support of this generalization.

It can then be argued that it is not inevitable that ES be interpreted as an "electronic bureaucracy." It is not necessarily so. To come back to our question: take out the bureau, the pen and the form and introduce the application, the device and the network, and things should change, should they not? Here we confront the new horizon of ES, and the kinds of imaginative solution that might make them still more significant. The point is that maybe, as much as anything else, our assumptions and history have constrained application of ES to date. We are back to mental models. It does not matter in whose head they reside; programmers, ES vendors, project managers, CEO's, or workers, the point is that very often, and so far, we have unwittingly rejected the chance to think more innovatively about processes. The overriding pressure in ES projects is to make the technology fit the host organization, and to achieve this through an intense process that operates within the tight box of a "project" that is organized to the apparent rationality of a "business case." Intrinsically this is limiting. Moreover, it relies heavily on the partial and dated understanding of all those involved in this rushed and pressured ES project. Again, what we see instead in the Long Conversation is the slow opening out of the debate and the realization that wider possibilities exist.

"Infusion" is an important concept. Infusion occurs when an innovation become incorporated within the organization's routine in a way that it is used to its full potential to increase business performance.[5] According to E. Rogers,[6] when the infusion stage is finished, the innovation process in an organization is complete. We define it as growth. What we see is that as businesses approach a higher level of growth, they begin to think more innovatively about the ES, starting to use its advanced features and being prepared to change what they do to exploit new possibilities. As they approach this level of infusion, they also establish a platform for future ES; they have

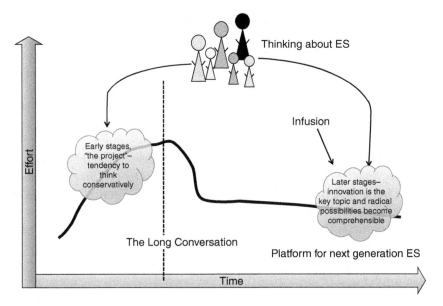

Figure 2.1 Infusion stage in the Long Conversation

new insight into the work that they do and how it might be organized. This is described pictorially in Figure 2.1. On the left hand side, in the official project stages, established mental models dominate. The general thinking among implementers, managers and users tends to be conservative. They try to make sure the process of implementation gives the organization the functionality that it currently understands. This is sensible, but by the time the right hand side is reached, a long process of social learning and sharing has unlocked some of the old assumptions, and there is a new appreciation of more novel ideas. There is more innovation and also, importantly, more preparedness for future innovation. The old organizational precepts, including bureaucracy and all that came with it, are more readily debated. We think there is evidence that businesses become much more open to radical new ideas about how work is done and how goals are achieved.

Origins and scope of enterprise systems

ES has its roots in the manufacturing industry and another related concept known as "Enterprise Resource Planning" or RP.[7] A number of authors then suggest that ERP is in turn an extension of Manufacturing Resource

Planning (MRP) or Materials Requirements Planning (MRP II). The name, ERP, is indeed a modification of MRP or MRP II, but this relationship between MRP, MRP II and ERP is not just a game of letters and initials. Manufacturing specialists have been credited as being pioneers in efforts of organizational integration. They sought systems that enabled the integration of tasks and technologies across the manufacturing processes, for example, from orders to materials to logistics. The need for this integration led to the development of packaged software, that is, software that could be bought by different companies who had similar needs to each other. From MRP in the 70s, through to the functionally more advanced MRP II in the 80s, and the development of the broader scope of ERP in the 90s, the integration dream has, reportedly, come true. The adoption of the term ES signifies that it is now enterprise-wide and generic to businesses everywhere, not just manufacturing industry.

As we noted earlier, orders, supply, payment and inventory are the staple fodder of ES. Typically, they have been described as "back-office" systems, automating business transactions that in turn supported client-facing and strategic activity. Increasingly, though, the modular extensions of ES have allowed them to become all encompassing, supporting the "front-office" of business intelligence (BI), e-business and CRM. BI applications take data from the ES database for analysis. These applications include data-warehouse, data-mining and decision support systems. CRM applications provide front-office solutions such as sales force automation or call-center support. Business-to-business (B2B) applications allow the company to integrate information beyond its own limits (inter-organizational integration). Such applications include solutions like e-procurement (to place orders to suppliers) and e-commerce (to receive orders from clients).

How do enterprise systems work?

ES enable the integration of business processes and associated data throughout an organization. Normally, the base of an ES is a single database that receives data from and to an associated set of modular applications. These modular applications support the different company functions. When new information is entered into a module, related information is automatically updated in the others. Early versions of ES-like systems ran on centralized mainframes. More typically, today's ES are designed for client-server architectures. Increasingly, however, ES are web-enabled, allowing access to systems from multiple and mobile locations. Beyond the web lies the cloud; a subtle extension of the concept embracing the idea of *always on, always available* services, provided as a utility.

The process of process

The classical difference between an ES and a more traditional information system is that when an organization adopts an ES, it does not design a new system to meet its extant or proposed ways of working. Instead, there is much greater emphasis on the organization adapting its business processes to the package's generic functionality. In other words, but only to some degree, they provide business processes "out of the box." Typically, the business implementing an ES will seek to rework its existing processes to a set of templates provided by the ES. The less customization that it requires of the ES, the more its approach is described as "vanilla." In the vernacular and practice of ES, a "vanilla" implementation is usually expected to be cheaper and more reliable.

Overall, configuring an ES encompasses two sets of decisions. First, companies have to decide which modules will be adopted, for example, finance and accounting modules, logistics modules. Second, they need to work through the modification options. The basic work is done through configuration tables. For example, these tables will set the basic company parameters – for example, country settings, tax settings and organizational unit settings. Then, a more detailed analysis of the functions of business processes themselves is needed. This optimizes between the system capabilities and the requirements expressed from within the business itself. Simple examples of this are that types of inventory accounting will be specified (first-in-first-out or last-in-first-out), the form of standard reports, and formulating available-to-promise logic.

Throughout this process, the adopting business relies on expertise from ES specialists. Invariably, this will be provided by the ES vendor itself or one of its approved partners. They provide the expertise for a complicated operation that seeks to mutually optimize the business process and the configuration of the software. The ES experts will be acutely conscious of when requirements conform to the base capabilities of the ES through its normal configuration, and when programmed customization is required. Customization increases cost both immediately and in the future as systems are maintained and upgraded. This process of customization is also known as "tailoring."[8] The term is useful because these adaptations blur the boundary between the "off-the-shelf" or "off-the-peg" metaphor of ES and the traditional, bespoke information system.

Most ES vendors have designed their systems to support what they claim to be "best-practice" processes. These practices reflect the experiences and suggestions of leading companies, and so we see a synergistic relationship between the ES vendor and its many customers; the former constantly learning from the latter, the latter then learning from the former. Sometimes, a company adopting ES for the first time is motivated by the chance to move to industry-standard and "best-practice" processes. It can be a motivator of sales, the new company often being attracted by the list of other companies that have already adopted the system.

Although relying on their work with industry leaders, ES vendors also look to academic theory (e.g., APICS) about the best way to do or manage some types of processes – for example, production floor or inventory control. The expertise thus developed becomes a key differentiator for the ES vendor, and these vendors are sometimes classified according to their strengths and experience with specific industries.

Although ES provides companies with broad functionality, companies often need to complement their ES with further applications. However broad the capability of ES is, a single ES rarely does it all. Consequently, bolt-on applications are offered by third-party providers. These bolt-on applications use the data from within the ES and are able to work in an integrated way with the basic ES package. They may, however, require some recoding in the ES or, at least, interface developments by using the ES's own toolset. Moreover, the fundamental philosophy behind ES is one of integration and so, as new bolt-on applications become popular, ES vendors work to make integration with them still easier. Sometimes this involves the ES vendor developing an alternative to rival a third-party bolt-on or, even, buying the supplier of these third-party applications. Many of today's key functions of ES started out as third-party bolt-on functionality, including SCM, B2B, CRM and BI.

Another way of developing the base capability of an ES is through the concept of "message brokering" or "middleware." Middleware allows disparate applications (either standalone packages or custom-built applications) to communicate through standardized messages. The technology eliminates the requirement that all modules share the same database. This integration approach is more flexible than implementing a standard ES. Hence, middleware is used when the motivation is to improve software integration as much as it is to improve software functionality. There are many notable applications of middleware, for example, Dell uses middleware architecture to handle finance and manufacturing functions. It also gives us another acronym to remember. When experts talk of building enterprise-wide capabilities through middleware integration, this perhaps involving one or more functions of a standard ES, they call this Enterprise Application Integration or EAI.

Business process reengineering

ES are often described as "process systems." We have talked of them implementing business processes and even being understood as "processes in a box." This focus on process opens up another aspect of ES. They are not just seen as being process systems in a pragmatic sense, but often also related to the idea of *a process philosophy* for business. What this idea of a process philosophy encompasses is that it is not just a case of providing a technology to support the everyday actions of business, as processes are as old as business itself, but that there are advantages to thinking about processes in a new way or with a new spirit. Most fundamentally, for two decades there has been an argument that businesses gain advantages if they organize around cross-functional processes rather than just building up a set of functions as in an organizational chart (we are talking about that pitchfork again). It is important here to note the idea of *cross-functional* processes. These are understood to be activities that integrate across the functional silos of the organization. It is not a case of building a warehousing system for the warehousing department. It is a case of building a process system that unites warehousing with logistics, materials supply, order processing, and even sales.

Here we are defining process as a set of logically related tasks performed to achieve a defined business outcome. From this perspective, processes have customers and they cross organizational boundaries.[9] The notion is popularly associated with Business Process Reengineering or BPR. This management concept is best traced to the work of Michael Hammer,[10] then Michael Hammer and James Champy[11] and, more or less contemporaneously, Thomas Davenport.[12] Basically, Hammers's observation at the start of the 1990s was that IT was being used to reconstruct traditional (i.e., bureaucratic) models of organization. In a memorable article for *Harvard Business Review*, he talked of the habit of embedding the "cowpaths" of the organization in silicon. He argued that IT presented a more fundamental opportunity, one that could support new models of organization. Most of all, he argued that the cross-functional process was key to understanding business value and the opportunities for efficiency. He provided a little evidence and some speculation to support his claim that order-of-magnitude benefits could follow from this way of thinking. His bold, striking paper was subtitled "Don't Automate, Obliterate."

In the years that followed, the concept of BPR was elevated by many management consultancies but, equally, criticized by many scholars.[13] For these scholars, BPR was simplistic, mechanistic and technologically deterministic. It ignored the subtle complexities of work, and the need to build successful teams and communities. It was also seen as being uncaring, of becoming the favourite excuse of those embarking on corporate restructuring and job-losses. It perhaps did not matter that Davenport had articulated a more rounded, though potentially less-radical, articulation of BPR, the topic that quickly became mired in controversy.

Later, Davenport would describe ES as the saviour of reengineering.[14] He argued that one of the major problems in supporting new organizational designs was to find process-oriented systems. As ES became popular, they were viewed as "processware," a conflation of "process" and "software." The integration philosophy and work structure of ES meant that they naturally supported a process-oriented organizational design, which remained the major premise of BPR. Indeed, Davenport's point is useful for it suggests how ES became the center of a general process philosophy in management and rode its way to becoming the norm for Fortune 500 companies, whether or not all scholars were ever going to approve of BPR itself.

Nowadays, the debate centers on the efficacy of ES itself. We have already circuited the main parts of the debate. There are questions of technological sophistication and whether ES are sufficiently flexible to enable organizations to adopt them easily and to innovate with them. Then there are questions of implementation process and, as we are highlighting here, the paradoxes and shortcomings of taking a short-term view of their implementation.

ES development lifecycle

Before ES, IS development had been understood as consisting of many activities in a Software Life Cycle (SLC). Typically, these activities include requirements gathering, design, testing and implementation. Some versions of the SLC describe these as following each other in a linear pattern but there are also important variations, including circular, iterative models. To scholars of these IS development approaches, ES are sometimes considered as a remarkable discontinuity.[15] This is because of the prepackaged approach meaning that the organization focuses on configuration instead of development. We have noted that when an organization adopts an ES, it does not design a new system to meet its extant or proposed ways of working. Consequently, ES change conventional understanding of the SLC in important ways.

The traditional SLC consists of activities performed by a company in the aim of developing, implementing and maintaining an IS for itself. It works for its own internal use. With ES, the model is different. Development occurs through two separate but related SLCs: adopters' activities and vendors' activities. In other words, again as we learned earlier, the vendors play a vital role in building best-practice models from across multiple ES cases. These are then configured through an internal process related to a single company. Brehm and Markus[16] call this the "Divided Software Life Cycle (DSLC) Model." The vendor is responsible for the original development of the ES, new releases and its upgrading. These responsibilities involve traditional activities of system analysis, design, coding and testing. The adopter is responsible for evaluating the ES in the concept phase, configuring it, rolling it out throughout the organization and using it. Furthermore, there is a continuous flow from the vendor to the adopter (e.g., releasing upgrades or new functionality) and near-continuous feedback from the adopter to the vendor (e.g., desired bug fixes and enhancements).

The impact of the DSLC on adopting businesses is very substantial in at least two main ways. First, these adopting companies require skills and roles that are different to those they developed for traditional IS. In particular, the ES team and users have to develop skills related to mapping organizational requirements, ES terminology, modeling business processes, and making choices about parameter configuration. The roles of users seem to change too. One study[17] found that users are deployed as an intelligence function, allowing managers to understand local issues as they moved an ES into each new site. The study called this "the finding of thorns." This user role is clearly different to, and more limited than, than that idealized by some authors for traditional IS (e.g., shaping requirements, designing processes and helping set the direction of the IS program).

Second, a long-term relationship emerges between the ES vendor and the adopter. With this, new challenges and opportunities appear for organizations. They have to handle and influence this relationship in a way that best achieves package maintenance, support and enhancement. Organizations maintain a dialogue that is mutually beneficial but also, potentially, fraught with difficulty. For the adopting organization, the creation of an internal ES support team usually follows. This team both maintains the external relationship and also builds their own skills so as to avoid an over-dependency.

Business value of enterprise systems

ES are the platforms of modern living. They are great, unseen utilities allowing supply and trade to occur in the modern age. Many of today's business practices could not happen without them; they have given us an inventory-light, just-in-time, networked and integrated age. It is probably a surprise to discover that the business value of ES is a controversial area. Despite the de-facto victory of adoption by the world's major corporations, different commentators have different opinions about the value of ES to these corporations and thence to the wider economy. Basically, the claimed benefits can be grouped into three key areas: The first is tackling IT problems and costs, the second is process efficiency, and the third is organizational effectiveness.[18]

In relation to IT, ES can solve many problems and costs in an organization. Historically, ES have been implemented by many companies to solve the year 2000 problem, to replace hard-to-maintain interfaces, to reduce software maintenance, to eliminate redundant data entry, to improve IT architecture, and consolidate multiple different systems of the same type (e.g., general ledger packages). In short, they are often chosen to solve the problems of an earlier generation of IT approaches based on discreet and tactical solutions. As many workers can testify, organizations in the early years of IT adoption have been dogged by data integration problems.

In relation to process, the ability of ES to integrate data and standardize processes can bring many improvements. These include faster cycle time, lower back-office staff requirements, reduced inventory, eliminated transactional errors, standardized business language and easier financial consolidation. Academic and industrial literature contains many examples and, given the scale of ES in society, reports are readily available. A good example is probably your local supermarket. All the big chains have precise and efficient inventory replenishment routines based on integrated data within the store and out into the supply-chain. Another example is AutoDesk, a manufacturer of computer-aided design software, and the report that this company reduced its delivery cycle time to customers from two weeks to twenty-four hours. The company also cut its financial closing time from twelve days to six. Nestle provides another case, saving US$ 325 million by using an ES. These reported savings relate to the reduction of inventory and distribution expenses. Detailed demand planning is a key part of this huge improvement.

There is also evidence related to improvements in organizational effectiveness beyond those gains through process efficiency. Such benefits include improved customer service, supporting business growth and improved access to information. Combining ES and the Internet, many companies have been able to offer self-service capabilities to customers and supply chain partners. These not only reduce processing costs but also, potentially, add to convenience, flexibility and knowledge. For example, Heineken gives its distributors access to information placed in its ES about product availability and sales options. Elsewhere, the implementation of an ES in a Latin American Internet Service Provider allowed the company to grow at less cost and with much greater rapidity. In less than six months, the company grew from ten thousand customers to more than one hundred thousand customers.[19]

The empirical evidence presented later in this book shows that higher benefits are positively related to the level of sophistication in the use of ES. Davenport also makes this point.[20] He suggests a two-dimensional framework for measuring the value creating potential of ES. He labels the first dimension as "the business domain." This refers to the general range of business locations in which an ES operates (from internal to the firm to the supply chain). The second dimension is labeled "the information scope" and refers to the level of information processing and analysis provided by the ES. Different categories of use emerge from this framework. The most basic use is the combination of transaction automation (information scope) with internal and individual processes (business domain). This is useful, he reports, but does not generate significant value. More effective use is the combination of process management (information scope) with supply chain processes (business domain). An example of this is the application of collaborative planning, forecasting and replenishment systems (CPFR) that allow supply-chain partners to share information on sales and production.[21]

Integrating all these ideas into the "Long Conversation," we see that returns on ES investment are achieved after a diligent process of learning and development of the ES's capabilities. Accordingly, higher levels of ES benefits are achieved when the ES capabilities are diffused throughout the organization (known as the osmosis factor), when the organization masters more sophisticated uses of the ES (referred to as the growth factor), and when the ES is dynamically modified to implement changes in the business model generated by the business environment (referred to as the adaptation factor). The outcome of osmosis, growth and adaptation leads the organization to achieve the highest possible benefits of an ES investment.

Economic and social consequences of enterprise systems

The broader question of the economic and social consequences of ES on industries, society and the world has been given surprisingly little attention.

However, the concern has been briefly considered by Davenport in his book: *Mission Critical: Realizing the Promise of Enterprise Systems.* Davenport bets on there being positive economic and social impacts of ES. He categorizes these into four expected effects. The first is greater productivity in advanced economies. He argues that, given that ES can allow companies to eliminate unneeded inventory, and that it can cut time and costs out of core business processes, companies and economies that make broad use of ES may increase their productivity more than those that do not. This is an advantage for developed economies. The second effect is interorganizational transformation. Davenport argues that companies implementing ES give themselves the foundations to create closer and more efficient relationships with customers and suppliers. The third effect is a new basis for competition in industries. As ES are becoming a common technology to every company in some industries (e.g., energy, automotive and high-tech), the basis for competition in these industries may change dramatically. According to Davenport's thesis, this is similar to that of the airline industry in 70s. When every airline had the same basic reservation systems, the same yield management systems, and similar frequent-flyer programs, the basis of competition changed. From this emerged a new battle for leadership in costs. The fourth effect is empowered employees. Davenport suggests that improvements in the organizational efficiency may mean that fewer employees are needed. He suggests that the surviving employees will be those whose have the broadest range of new abilities. He notes that the learning process associated with this will be beneficial for the society, but it will nonetheless be difficult to accomplish.

Conclusions

With their great scale and their great penetration into business markets, ES are arguably a great, unseen utility. They provide the information exchange and processes that make modern businesses work. They have not been uncontroversial, as we have noted, but neither are they a fixed and finished concept. Information Technology in the business world is ES, and ES continues to develop and change. So, we should be alert to the long-term learning effects of individual businesses as they make their journey with ES. As Figure 2.1 tells us, we see in the Long Conversation that infusion, and a greater preparedness to be innovative, follows late in a learning process. The mental models of the old organization are only slowly eroded but, when they are, there is a willingness to think anew about the functionality offered by ES. More advanced features are adopted. Moreover, we believe, the limitations of existing ES are more readily seen, and there is an increased demand for something potentially new and innovative.

Learning is not confined to individual businesses. They are not walled cells. Instead, through the DSLC and other mechanisms such as supply-chain, learning carries over and across industry as a whole. When this is understood, the long Conversation can be seen as recursive and layered. It is not just that businesses erode old models and approach a more innova-tive standpoint on their own. Partnerships, sectors and even industry itself also moves. Thus, after 20 years of ES, we argue that we are approaching a point of new and profound innovation, a theme we return to in Chapter 6. The same learning processes that promote infusion in individual compa-nies will eventually erupt into pan-industrial innovation. It is a tectonic effect of all the adoption processes of all the organizations.

CHAPTER 3

Biological evolution: Osmosis, growth and adaptation

The "Long Conversation" comprises three vital points of learning and development. Each point tends to create emergent complexity that can set the implementation back and reorient it away from its original focus and motivate more group-learning. They are as follows: osmosis, growth and adaptation (see Figure 3.1). Placing these three vital points together is what makes for information technology mastery, something that relies on the formal and informal sharing of knowledge about technology and the affected processes and structures.[1]

Osmosis

Osmosis is a concept used in chemistry and biology to describe the movement of a solvent through a membrane that separates solutions of different concentrations. For example, when referring to water, osmosis is effectively the diffusion of water molecules. In other words, osmosis can be understood as the situation in which something is dissolved in something else.[2] The application of this concept to Enterprise System (ES) allows us to talk about ES osmosis as the passage of an enterprise system from a business area where it is highly concentrated to a business area where concentration is lower. In an ES environment, the osmosis factor involves both the implementation of a new ES functionality into additional business functions or processes, and the rollout of a particular ES function already implemented in some part of the corporation into other business units. This creates systemic lag or delay, often dressed up as "employees not being up to speed," but without giving them ways of learning. Such ES enhancements might be preplanned or arise out of organizational learning once the ES is in use. For instance, the case evidence reveals that when the companies under study felt they had satisfied their original needs and objectives, new objectives and ideas emerged. Thus osmosis follows an iterative process.

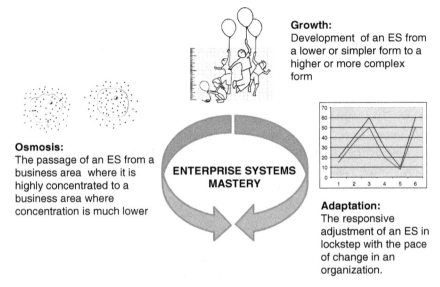

Growth:
Development of an ES from a lower or simpler form to a higher or more complex form

Osmosis:
The passage of an ES from a business area where it is highly concentrated to a business area where concentration is much lower

ENTERPRISE SYSTEMS MASTERY

Adaptation:
The responsive adjustment of an ES in lockstep with the pace of change in an organization.

Figure 3.1 Long Conversation's three vital points

Source: This figure has been taken from O. Lorenzo, P. Kawalek, and B. Ramdani, "Long Conversation: Learning How to Master Enterprise Systems," *California Management Review*, 53 (1), Fall 2009.

Seeing osmosis in practice

We see the detail of how osmosis works in many of the cases. Frequently, it shows up as a continual stream of projects as new functionality and new users enter the process.

The UK charity worked to share four ES modules among its 850 staff. It was intended that the process be quick, but it became hampered by the fact that the organization did not have documented processes. Remedies were sought by introducing new business analysis tasks and carefully introducing the different modules to different teams. Project plans were recast many times. The engineering company in Latin America provides further evidence of this. When managers were thought to have satisfied their original needs and objectives, new objectives and ideas emerged. As the CEO of this engineering company stated:

> Our ES implementation objectives have moved depending on our needs; first we needed urgently the automation and consolidation of our financial processes throughout the corporation, then the remaining processes were evaluated. Now we are evaluating the possibility of implementing the ES in the project and operations processes.

The ES support manager in the same company also pointed out:

> New needs are stated annually; based on this, an annual plan is released, which defines the functionalitiy to be implemented or rolled out over the next months.

Thus, ES implementation in the engineering company unfolded over time. There were similar patterns in the coffee company. The system's sales and distribution module was initially installed in the factory. In the second year, it was initially planned to be undertaken in one of the regional centers as a pilot project. Two years later, it started to be diffused throughout the rest of the 12 remote regions around the country (see Box 3.1). The CEO put it like this:

> This decision was mainly influenced by the industrial environment whereby competition and high-demanding customers were pushing toward excellence. Real time information was critical for facing the competition and meeting the clients' needs.

Growth

ES are complex and many of their most vaunted benefits depend on expert use. Users can master them only after some time and even then, often in what follows the form of a staircase. All this means is that some functions tend to be mastered earlier than others. Three of the cases show this. A typical pattern is to master transaction automation and decision support much earlier than process management automation and performance monitoring. These latter activities seem to depend on mastery of the former. One implication of this is that organizations lose time and effectiveness by pursuing the various benefits in the wrong order, and they fail to realize how important it is for users to develop expertise for the systems to attain the highest business value.

The analysis and comparison of the cases allowed the authors to identify a similar pattern of introduction of ES capabilities (see the definition of these capabilities in Box 3.2). Initially, the transaction automation capability and the decision-making process support capability were introduced simultaneously over the first year. Coordination and customer service capability were then introduced. Finally, capabilities giving performance monitoring and process management automation were introduced. This emergent ES growth pattern is also supported by evidence from previous literature.[3]

Box 3.1 The case of Coffee Company: diffusing the sales and distribution functionality through 12 regional centers

The diffusion of the ES into 12 sales and distribution (S&D) regional centers located nationwide was prioritized by the Coffee's CEO. These centers received finished goods from the factory, stored them in the warehouse, sold, invoiced and collected money from local small markets and large retailers. Three key human resources were allocated to implement this initiative. It was led by the S&D manager who became the nominated key user. Two other employees were assigned to play the role of change agents, who were trained on the functionality for three months in the corporate offices. Given the wide scope and complexity expected for this initiative, the key user committee and the CEO made the decision of allocating enough resources for undertaking this task. The three resources had previous experience implementing an ES with their former employers a few years earlier. The S&D key user was in charge of this diffusion journey. He had the goal of standardizing the processes of his 12 S&D regional centers. He had suffered the organizational chaos of managing 12 silos for many years.

It was initially planned that the project would be piloted in one of the regional distribution centers. The implementation took about four weeks, including system configuration, testing and training. The key user monitored the project through the use of a project Gantt and follow-up meetings took place on a weekly basis. Once the system was up and running in the S&D center, the change agents started coaching, guiding and transferring knowledge to final users. The change agents and the designated ES consultants for the pilot project were in place for two weeks to stabilize the system and solve any problem that arose. After two weeks, an internal help desk took the role of giving remote support to final users. The two change agents were part of this help desk. The idea was to encourage users to ask questions and uncover doubts related to a recent implementation in specific areas. In addition, analysis of these questions allowed key users to know what new training should be developed or if the system required fine-tuning. They recognized that most inquiries coming from the centers were related to procedures and norms, rather than system issues. They developed and wrote a procedure manual to help final users in the S&D centers to use the system.

After the successful diffusion of the system in the first S&D center, the key user started the implementation of the plan Gantt for the remaining regional centers. The plan was scheduled for implementing the system in each regional center one after the other. The whole implementation took about 18 months. While the change agents were implementing in one center, they were also supporting the centers already using the system through the help desk.

Source: See O. Lorenzo, P. Kawalek, and B. Ramdani, "The Diffusion of Enterprise Systems within Organizations: A Social Learning Theory Perspective," in *Proceedings of the 16th European Conference on Information Systems,* Galway, Ireland, 2008.

The pattern can be observed by considering organizations that ascend a three-step staircase of growth (see Figure 3.2). The operational level refers to the use of the ES for basic activities, such as transaction processing and producing reports for day-to-day decision-making. The effectiveness level occurs when companies achieve the kind of business integration that leverages tighter coordination among discrete business activities, enabling them to serve their customers effectively. The intelligence level implies acting on data in two ways. First, ESs can be used for managing processes by incorporating business rules and the heuristics previously used manually – that is, process management automation. Second, ESs can be used to transform data into knowledge through analytical capabilities – that is, monitoring performance. As the organization ascends the staircase of ES mastery, it achieves a more aggregated and sophisticated use of the ES.[6]

Seeing growth in practice

The brewery company aimed for a "big bang" strategy so as to complete a conversion to ES as quickly as possible. They wanted to implement a total of seven modules in the same project. However, to achieve this, and as user requirements emerged, they began to customize the system. Moreover, it became apparent that even where implementation was successfully achieved, full potential was not being reached. The project then began to focus on getting the best out of the system, using it in increasingly

Box 3.2 Enterprise systems capabilities

Transaction Automation	This refers to the use of the ES to automate business transactions in order to perform them with more uniformity and control (e.g., processing data in an integrated and standardized manner, standardized flow of work, transaction control using business rules, and tracking transactions and data).
Decision-making Support	This capability comprises business decision-making based on data provided by the ES (e.g., data outputs and reporting options).
Coordination	Coordination is seen as a response to problems caused by interdependencies.[4] Typical interdependencies that may be handled by the ES are those defined as "share resource" and "producer-consumer" (e.g., share resource can be seen as sharing the same body of information between different departments or business units that require it simultaneously. Producer-consumer is concerned with synchronizing activities or processes embedded in a value chain so that the resource required by the consumer is available when needed).
Customer Service	This capability comprises the use of ES to provide differentiated and customized services to both internal and external clients (e.g., an ES may support easier and speedier ordering by customers).
Monitoring Performance	This capability comprises the recording and monitoring of performance indicators. Typically this is achieved through management information tools, which give direct access to the key performance indicators of a company.
Process management automation	This capability comprises the automation of administrative processes. That is, it is the ability of the ES to act on data by incorporating business rules based on the heuristic procedure previously used by specialists[5] (e.g., MRP [Materials Requirements Planning] and DRP [Distribution Requirements Planning] are examples of management techniques supported by ES).

Source: O. Lorenzo and P. Kawalek, "A Model of Enterprise Systems Infusion," in *Proceedings of the European Operations Management Association (Euroma) Conference*, INSEAD, France, 2004.

sophisticated ways. A business manager described how his own role had changed:

> We were trying to use it more and more effectively … that philosophy extended to both the business and to the systems … I moved to more of a general strategic role rather than a technology driven role, trying to see what other opportunities existed by having a fresh pair of eyes looking at all areas.

Meanwhile in Latin America, the growth of the ES in the coffee company was a cumulative process over time. Over four years of ES use, the implementation process progressed with the addition of new functionality and capabilities (see Table 3.1). In the first year, the company focused on automating transactions and some limited use of reports. Over the following three years, the company continued automating transactions throughout the organization by adding areas such as regional warehouses, sales centers and transport operations. The decision-making process support was extensively deployed in several areas over the same period. Consequently, these two capabilities penetrated in cumulative fashion over a period of four years. At the same time as this process progressed, coordination,

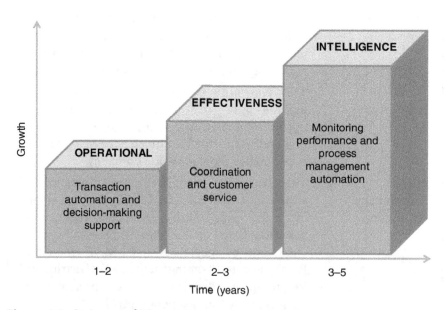

Figure 3.2 Staircase of ES mastery

Source: This figure has been taken from O. Lorenzo, P. Kawalek, and B. Ramdani, "Long Conversation: Learning How to Master Enterprise Systems," *California Management Review*, 53 (1), Fall 2009.

Table 3.1 ES growth factor in the Coffee Company

Year	Operational	Effectiveness	Intelligence
1	Limited use of reports by the ES. Use of Excel for reporting ES-related data. Transaction automation in financial accounting and administrative tasks, Coffee purchasing in remote facilities and its integration to the production plan, processing of production batches and its integration into the cost accounts procedure.		
2	Use of the ES for reporting its own data related to finance, IT and manufacturing. Transaction automation for the entering and recording of IT service orders, and sales processes in one of the 12 regions.	Use of the ES for entering service orders into the IT department: (easier and faster ordering for end-users). Purchasing department and external accounting users can share the same information.	
3	Use of the ES for reporting its own data related to sales and inventories in all regions. Use of the ES for reporting specific data required by senior management. Use of the ES for transaction automation in the sales processes in the remaining 11 regions.	The closing of monthly financial accounts was reduced to three days due to integration. By having products picked up twice a week instead of once a week, the stock turnover in intermediaries' trucks augmented. The finished goods warehouse could see the regional stock levels and issue more accurate and prompt replenishment orders. Stock cycle dropped from ten to seven days.	Monitoring performance of costs and return on operations in each region. Monitoring sales performance of intermediaries and final retailers' accounts receivable.

Continued

Table 3.1 Continued

Year	Operational	Effectiveness	Intelligence
4	Use of the ES for reporting its own data related to DRP and purchasing. Transaction automation in the processes related to (1) the operation and maintenance of distribution trucks (transport operations) and (2) the entering and recording of IT service orders in the remote facilities.	Regional centers introduce service orders into the IT department (easier ordering). Intermediaries provided with data about their own sales, accounts receivable, stocks and visits. e-orders received from large clients (easier and faster ordering for clients). Coordination allowed a reduction in stock levels from seven to three days	Use of DRP technique. Monitoring sales budget using Excel and Visual Basic and by importing data from the ES Monitoring KPIs using the management information functionality

Source: Adapted from Lorenzo, O., P. Kawalek and B. Ramdani, "Long Conversation: Learning how to master enterprise systems", *California Management Review*, 53 (1), Fall 2009.

customer service and performance monitoring capabilities developed from the second year, and process management automation in the fourth year. Coordination, customer service, and performance monitoring were also incorporated within the organization's routine year by year, again in cumulative fashion, adding areas each year.

As mentioned earlier, we clearly observed this pattern of growth of ES capabilities in three cases. Although a similar pattern was identified across these, each site exhibited different timings of growth (see Figure 3.3). Two specific examples reveal this. First, regarding the number of capabilities incorporated at a particular time, the three sites presented different rates of progress. Coffee Company needed four years to incorporate all six capabilities, Engineering needed five years, and Chemical needed seven years (see Figure 3.3). Second, we can see that the number of business areas affected by each capability was increasing year by year for Coffee Company and Engineering, but Chemical was not able to deploy the first two capabilities in further areas between years 1 and 4 (see circles of the first two capabilities in Chemical of Figure 3.3).

During these first four years in Chemical, the ES implementation was focused on a narrow project for the areas of sales administration and finance. A number of negative factors affected the project over this period. Perhaps, the most significant of these was that consultants led the project with only scarce participation from key users and senior managers. This resulted in a very low level of learning for the organization. Consultants completed the project, but Chemical was unable to grow beyond that. We could say that the ES implementation was managed from a traditional project management approach driven by time and cost reduction. Eventually, ES was up and running, but at the expense of the greater learning experience. The implementation struggled. Between years 4 and 5, Chemical restarted the implementation of the ES into the rest of business areas. The implementation strategy was now radically different. They learnt the lesson and started a new implementation process based on a long-term perspective, with a stronger emphasis on learning.

Osmosis is necessary for growth to happen

After seeing the evidence from cases of how osmosis and growth worked, we argue that osmosis is necessary for growth to happen. Mastering an ES evolves as a reciprocal action and reaction of its elements: osmosis, growth and adaptation. Here we describe this interaction of osmosis and growth.

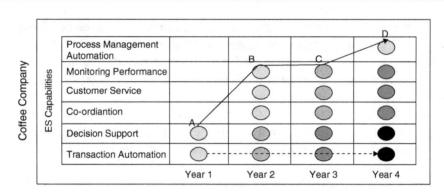

Dashed Line and Circles: moving horizontally into right in any row allows reading how a specific ES capability was incorporated. Stronger black grade inside the circles from one cell to the next implies that the capability was incorporated in further area or unit in that given year.

Solid Line: The ES Capabilites' Total Growth Process

Figure 3.3 A comparison of the staircase of growth in three cases

Source: This figure has been taken from O. Lorenzo, P. Kawalek, and B. Ramdani, "Long Conversation: Learning How to Master Enterprise Systems," *California Management Review*, 53 (1), Fall 2009.

Transaction automation is the first capability incorporated and used (growth), see Table 3.1. That is, once any ES functionality is implemented, the application of the system for recording and tracking of data is immediate. After this, in all sites studied, users from individual areas began asking information to manage their daily operations. This implied the use of reports and data outputs from the system meaning that decision-making process support was incorporated. The coordination capability is incorporated (growth) after two or more ES functionalities are implemented or a specific set of functionalities is rolled out into two or more business areas (osmosis). Coordination is possible only as the result of the integration of two or more ES modules (e.g., purchasing and manufacturing in the Coffee Company, see Table 3.1) or the integration of two or more business units (e.g., regional warehouses and the finish-goods warehouse in Coffee, see Table 3.1). This enables the management of the business on the basis of a single, integrated set of corporate data.

Business integration through osmosis also originates through the incorporation of customer service capability. As has been argued by a number of authors, business integration brings about better customer service. Such business integration facilitates reduced cycle times and synchronized processes, which is translated into improved customer service. It follows that the effectiveness use (growth) requires integration (osmosis), which occurs after the operational level of growth is achieved in individual areas or business units. Then, a precedence constraint exists.[7]

Similar results have been found in supply chain environments.[8] Effective use of enterprise systems in a supply chain can be seen as the joint management of decisions in a network of interrelated firms (e.g., joint decision with supplier on topics like planning of demand management). This level of use implies the process integration of these interrelated firms through ERP systems and specialized SC functionality (e.g., demand planning and forecasting, warehouse management systems and transport management systems). The combination of these systems is known as supply chain-centric enterprise systems. Then, the joint management of decision capability is incorporated (growth) after a set of ERP and Supply Chain functionalities are implemented or rolled out into two or more different interrelated firms (osmosis). In addition, the maximum value creation is achieved when the interrelated firms use their enterprise systems to automate advanced inventories practices (e.g., classification practices, vendor managed inventory and forecasting models). In other words, by diffusing the enterprise system beyond the organization's frontiers (osmosis) and using advanced inventory practices (growth – process management automation capability), companies in the supply chain are able to make better joint decisions (growth).

Adaptation

Faced with the upheaval of an ES project, organizations will typically strive to return to "normal" as quickly as possible. In fact, normality, or rather the original perception of it, never returns. The learning associated with system-use, the processes of spreading and mastery, the changes generated by the business environment, and the technical updates brought by manufacturers, mean that a constant stream of functional and technical adaptations are sought. Adaptation means modification and adjustment of an ES in use in a given setting.

This becomes the new reality. To choose between alternative functional and technical adaptations, different coping strategies are adopted. Sometimes judgments are made as to the strategic value of different adaptation requests; however, in other cases managers seek to limit demands for change by neglecting some requests or instituting teams of users to make these judgments.

This adaptation factor is crucial in highly dynamic business environments in which organizations frequently have to adapt their business models in order to add value derived from their ES investment. Our evidence is in line with the argument that enterprise systems are flexible technological infrastructures that allow evolution from legacy business models to new ones.[9] The lesson is that this may be a new norm and an ongoing commitment.[10]

Seeing adaptation in practice

The telecom company implemented an ES in Europe. After starting with the e-procurement tool, its Spanish subsidiary went through two unpredictable adaptation stages: evolution into a regional procurement platform and finally into a global pan-European procurement unit. The ES was adapted over time to the different needs triggered by environmental stimuli. First, the subsidiary implemented the system as an enabler for control in the Materials, Repairs and Operations (MRO) procurement process. In the first adaptation stage (see Box 3.3), in response to the telecom market downturn in 2000, the system was diffused into the Iberia Market Unit (Portugal and Spain) as an enabler of shared services for the purchase-to-pay process. This centralization allowed the company to further reduce the number of purchasing employees throughout the area, to reduce costs of the purchase-to-pay process by an average of 30 percent, and to build up a network of regional suppliers. The new shared service model meant modifications for the ES in use in the Spanish subsidiary and the rollout of the e-procurement tool into the Portuguese operation. In the second adaptation stage, the tele-com company implemented a global and centralized e-procurement model designed to reduce costs worldwide. This entailed outsourcing services to a Nordic marketplace for the activities of supplier activation, content management and integration with suppliers. The new global business model allowed the company to develop a network of global suppliers and to obtain greater visibility throughout the whole process. In addition, the new global model meant significant adjustments for the ES in use in the Iberia Market Unit.

Going through these adaptation stages, the ES had to be reconfigured and modified based on the changing requirements of each stage. Over a period of four years in the telecom sector, the ES was used to give the company flexibility to implement different business models and strategies. The ES vendor worked to help the company to achieve this challenge through the continuous upgrading of the e-procurement functionality. Indeed, introducing functional changes into the system would have been impossible without the continuous technical and functional upgrading of the system by the vendor.

Further evidence of ES adaptation comes from the engineering company, where a merger of some operations with a parent company led to a substantial reconfiguration of the ES settings. After using the first configuration of the system's time recording process, users found a serious gap between the modeled process and the process as performed. This mismatch motivated a learning and improvement exercise. The various improvements and adjustments to the ES, processes, and procedures, were realized to improve the data quality and reduce the processing and delivery time. Evidence from an internal document shows how the adaptation approach operated here. A set of improvements was carried out: easier data entry through the reduction of options in the ES; implementing validations to run for the detection of mistakes in data entry; running transaction "jobs" daily to feed the information needs of corporate projects and remove the need for local databases; implementing validations in the transfer process. This involved the creation of a query to compare the data inside the temporal database with the data transferred into the application database. Before this improvement was made, mistakes were only found when encountered by users, and the tracking and fixing of errors had become very time-consuming. Decentralizing the Center for Timesheet Processing from corporate headquarters to remote offices followed then, as did the implementation of electronic timesheets and a workflow system.

When seeing adaptation in practice, it is critical to recognize the importance of process modeling for the modification and adjustments of an ES in use. Both in Engineering and Telecom, process modeling was deployed

Box 3.3 First adaptation stage in Telecom: preparing for market deceleration

Context: In 2001, the dot.com bubble burst, an event that can be attributed to unfulfilled expectations. It also affected telecommunication companies that had invested heavily in new licenses for the new third generation services that were supposed to be launched in 2001. Investments had to be cut dramatically in the face of new market realities. Although Telecom continued to pursue a global decentralized strategy, the company began to consolidate some of the support processes in shared services. The aim was to create a more adaptable and flexible business model that permitted economies of scale and scope. Execution of this strategy entailed creating Business Support Centers (BSCs) for the countries in Western Europe, a decision that affected 17 subsidiaries. The BSCs used shared services for administrative, financial and purchasing processes. The new business model brought significant changes in Telecom's structure and culture. The administrative, financial and purchasing processes were consolidated in two hubs for Western Europe. Subsidiaries defined new roles and were responsible for the internal customer relationship management. This model also meant that Telecom developed a service culture in back-office departments. Given that the expectations in the telecom market changed from an optimistic scenario to conservative. Telecom wanted to create a more flexible and adaptable business model that would be able to react to any external contextual change. A study revealed high operating costs due to the duplication of resources across all subsidiaries through its decentralized model. The company subsequently developed a market unit solution whereby it unified applications in all the subsidiaries. The market unit solution was based on a former SAP implementation and incorporated the implementation of the SAP B2B functionality as the enabler of consolidated purchase-to-pay processes.

The Implementation of the Electronic Purchase-to-Pay Process: The implementation of the SAP B2B functionality into the purchase-to-pay process was a European initiative. The project was called electronic purchase-to-pay, or just ep2p, and it became a key enabler of the BSC initiative. One of the BSCs was established in Madrid to manage Portugal and Spain. The upgraded functionality (EBP) was used for this initiative. The modeling of the to-be purchase-to-pay process borrowed from the process already implemented in Spain. This reference process took into account minor requirements from other countries just as France and Holland and was redesigned to create a core model that became the standard for countries participating in BSC initiatives. The implementation of ep2p and the creation of the BSCs took 6 months in all. The ep2p project consisted mainly of the migration of the former functionality to the new version (EBP). In Spain, a good communication campaign was required to explain to users the need to migrate from one version to another, even though the former version had only recently been implemented. The project was led by the local purchase area and was supported by well-known global consulting firm, who then rolled out the system to the other European BSCs. This initiative focused on the transactional elements of the purchasing processes. For EE, there were no significant changes in the way they carried out the purchasing process. The main change was the introduction of a new role called Service Manager in the subsidiaries, responsible for the service management of the purchase-to-pay process. Given that Spain was one of the places were a BSC was established, the purchasing personnel remained the same as before. From a technological perspective, this initiative consisted of merely migrating from one version to another, the second of which included better materials classification functionality. From a process and technological perspective, there were no significant changes in the way suppliers interacted with Telecom. However, the new initiatives did imply some major changes in organizational structure. Telecom asked suppliers to take on the responsibility of the cataloguing process. Training programs were needed to achieve this objective. Once implementation was complete, the company and suppliers adapted quickly to the new processes.

Consequences: For Telecom, this initiative meant that it began to lose independence in the design and execution of local back-office processes. The new consolidated purchase-to-pay process allowed the corporationto have more visibility of spending and more control over the operation. This initiative allowed the company an additional 30 percent process costs reduction: (1) suppliers had to catalogue all their materials into the system; (2) suppliers developed internal cataloguing capabilities; and (3) some local suppliers began to develop the capacity to deliver in more than one country.

Source: See O. Lorenzo and A. Diaz, "Enterprise Systems as an Enabler of Fast-Paced Change: The Case of Global B2B Procurement in Ericsson," in C. Ferran and R. Salim, ed., *Enterprise Resource Planning for Global Economies: Managerial Issues and Challenges*, edited by (Hershey, PA: Information Science Reference, 2008).

from the beginning to ensure the clear documentation of the organizational needs and to support bridging the gap between the new / changed process demands and the ES functionality (see Box 3.4).

Box 3.4 Process modeling: a fundamental tool for adaptation

Process modeling is found to correlate significantly with better enterprise systems implementation results in the long term. Process modeling is a technique that allows organizations to make their process knowledge explicit. Process modeling includes a vast set of methodologies, techniques and tools used for process mapping, process analysis, process measurement, process (re)design, and process training, among others. Putting this in a slightly more simple way, process modeling helps to generate an accurate representation of the current process (as-is modeling) and to model the new process as the company wishes it to be run (to-be modeling). Process modeling combines concepts and tools from other areas of business practice, in particular quality management, business process reengineering and software development.

Process modeling is often used by consultants and adopting companies during the implementation of enterprise systems. It is relevant for system configuration because the models describe process activities, business rules, organizational roles and other issues that must be configured in the system. Process modeling is also used as a very helpful tool for matching the company requirements to system functionality.

Evidence from many real cases suggests the widespread use of process modeling as a preparatory exercise before the enterprise system implementation begins in earnest. The use of process modeling before the implementation is reported to ensure better long-term results for the implementation. Process modeling before implementation allows companies to carefully understand and define business process requirements and align them to company needs and strategies. Thus, it is an introspective analysis that companies do before the interaction with ES vendors. Doing the opposite is like building a house with the roof first.

Source: See more detailed information about the impact of process modeling on ES implementation in A. Diaz, O. Lorenzo, and B. Claes, "ERP Implementation Strategies: The Importance of Process Modeling and Analysis," in *Enterprise and Organizational Modeling and Simulation 2010 Conference (EOMAS)*, Tunisia 2010.

Adaptation reinforces osmosis and growth

After seeing the evidence of how adaptation worked for Telecom and Engineering, we argue that adaptation reinforces osmosis and growth. The Spanish subsidiary of Telecom became one of the pioneer European users in the development of an electronic procurement model enabled by an ES. This development meant the implementation of new functionality on an additional process (osmosis) after using ES for the previous 4 years. The new procurement functionality allowed purchasing staff to take advantage of the operational capabilities of the ES (growth). This also allowed other areas (e.g., accounts payable area) to improve the integration and coordination among Finance and Purchasing departments (i.e., growth – effectiveness capability). After a certain period, regional managers identified the opportunity of reducing costs by implementing a shared service business model for Portugal and Spain. This meant changes in processes, roles, and, of course, the system. The new business model resulted in the reconfiguration of the system for the Spanish subsidiary. At the same time, the adaptation of the system for the subsidiary gave rise to a better internal integration in telecom because two different subsidiaries could jointly operate for the management of the purchase-to-pay process. In other words, the reconfiguration of the system in Spain (adaptation) allowed Telecom to improve the coordination among multinational users (growth). The reconfiguration (adaptation) also modified the system to allow the diffusion of new functionality (osmosis) to Portugal for work under a centralized business model. Osmosis (rollout into Portugal) and growth (more advanced use of the system) were here driven by the adaptation of the system (reconfiguration in Spain).

Conclusions

Key points

- The enterprise system implementation is a continuous adoption and diffusion process based on three vital points of learning and development: osmosis, growth and adaptation.
- Osmosis involves both the implementation of a new ES functionality into additional business functions or processes, and the rollout of a particular ES function already implemented in some part of the corporation into other business units.

- Growth refers to the development of an enterprise system from a lower or simpler form to a higher or more complex form. This is based on expert use of the system. Enterprise system capabilities are mastered step by step; some are mastered earlier than others. A typical pattern of growth is to master transaction automation and decision support capabilities earlier than coordination and customer service capability. The more aggregated and sophisticated uses related to monitoring performance and process management automation capabilities are mastered after a certain level of maturity.
- Adaptation means modification and adjustment of an ES in use in a given setting. This factor is crucial in highly dynamic business environments in which organizations frequently have to adapt their business models to add value derived from their ES investment
- Mastering an enterprise system evolves as a reciprocal action and reaction of its elements: osmosis, growth and adaptation. Osmosis is necessary for growth to happen, adaptation reinforces osmosis and growth.

Practical implications

- Enterprise systems should be seen as being part of a long journey, our Long Conversation, based on a continuous implementation, diffusion and assimilation of knowledge.
- ES value depends on the actual usage of the system, which is developed over time by mastering the different levels of ES capabilities (growth).

CHAPTER 4

Mastery is a long conversation

The analysis of osmosis, growth and adaptation shows that the whole process is more complex, more variable and longer than originally anticipated. Ultimately, it constitutes a challenge to the prior culture of the organization. This begins to change in some surprising ways. Knowledge-sharing, support and expertise become key to progress. Teams from different parts of the organization come together to solve difficult problems. In some cases, new structures emerge or specialist teams develop. The organization keeps talking; it keeps on having to talk. This ongoing, developing conversation can be understood as the pursuit of "mastery." Much of this is captured by Engestrom's notion of "knotworking," wherein teams form around particular cross-organizational issues and concerns.[1] Through these, linkages are made with prior evolutions of business in history, when earlier generations of technology challenged an organizational orthodoxy. When this happened, the need to build specialist knowledge of that new technology became a focus of organizational development.

The longitudinal evidence of our cases shows that attaining this mastery of the system becomes increasingly the central concern of the mission, as teams try to discover more capabilities. As this happens, new organizational norms and teams nurture and share the specialist knowledge relating to the Enterprise System (ES) itself. Years after the initial training programs have ceased, we see the emergence of key knowledge nodes, and even guild-like structures in the organization. This wave then ripples beyond the immediate concerns of the ES and into broader process and organizational improvement and transformation. Perhaps, this is why the most surprising things tend to become obvious to users in retrospect. At the outset, this was never acknowledged. It was never planned for. Perhaps, managers never expected it to be like this.

Seeing mastery in practice

Across all the cases, often amid the pain and frustration of failed or slipping project delivery, there comes a decoupling point in which organizations abandon formal project plans and instead institute a more open-ended learning process. This is nicely illustrated in the oldest of the eight cases, the Coffee Company. This company first implemented ES following a traditional implementation approach by focusing on discrete projects aimed at adopting defined functionalities in specific business areas. To achieve this, they organized themselves into a project team composed of seven internal staff and some external consultants. They saw it as a project with a beginning and an end, just like any other project. Then, the company changed its view to adopt a long-term perspective, encouraging a new pattern of learning based on key-users' experiences. No phases were stated. The company now talked of an endless process composed of an infinite number of projects.

Another case resonates with this. After five years, the Engineering Company reported that only two of the planned business areas had been automated; finance and human resources. Even then, these areas were only partially developed. At the time the CFO argued:

> The human resources area is behind; ... they have only automated the payroll, but training and personnel assessment are delayed; ... this fact is not good if one considers that we are a professional services company.

It was this crisis of confidence that led Engineering to seek new ways of user-learning and sharing from which it would eventually achieve more successful osmosis and growth.

Meanwhile, the Brewery was encountering similar difficulties and focused the project on restricted areas of functionality. According to business managers, performance remained disappointing for many years, and many technical adaptations were sought. Eventually the very process of seeking these adaptations promoted new conversations in the organization and better outcomes were achieved.

The IT Company provides a contrasting case. It is a business that implemented ES on a worldwide scale and across a range of functions. It was the only one of our cases in which the original implementation ran to time and budget. The original investigation looked at its use of methodology, reporting how the "participative" ethos of one of its project managers was, in fact, used to keep the project consistent with his priorities and timescale.

The case was revisited after six years. An Accounts Business Manager was asked directly about the original project. He replied:

> When we look back now, what we thought was the end was actually the beginning. We've had a lot to do since then.

In a detail to a supplementary question, he added:

> ... but there was a lot of celebration then. You know, the fact that we'd come in on time and done a lot of work quickly. That was worth it in a way. We got to know each other better and we enjoyed working better as a result.

He went on to elaborate saying that he did not attribute this additional enjoyment to the system itself, but to the fact that its installation had taken the team through a shared experience and that working-relations were better as a result:

> I am not sure we always knew what the other teams were doing, the sales teams for example. But, I've got to know them personally over the years. This is because of the ES project. We just ended up putting faces to names and being able to say hello when we met up. ... We can easily discuss problems now. Not just with sales, but with other teams like manufacturing.... When people say that ES improves communication, I only sort of agree – it does, but only partly because of the system itself. That's the smaller part of it, actually. The main thing is learning the processes.

We found that as well as the formal "'user" meetings, the ES was also discussed and developed through "client group meetings." These were staff meetings not directly concerned with the ES project. Their remit was to discuss client issues. Although this formal remit was client management, according to a senior accountant, there is "nothing in the ES that does not relate to a client in some way." All staff participated in these groups, with around 20 groups meeting weekly. They often had representation from outside (e.g., sales). Hence, they were the focus for debate among the team members about the use of the ES. Moreover, evidence was presented that the client groups considered issues relating to contractors as well; in short, almost anything concerned with the operation of the division. Sources reported that ES tips and knowledge would be exchanged at these meetings that would last anything from 20 minutes to one hour.

> There will always be something to do with the ES, at least for a few minutes" reported the senior accountant, "and sometimes it takes the whole meeting.

Frequently, one member of staff would be invited to present issues related to processes or technical features. According to an accounts manager:

> "The Clients Groups are our quality circles. If there's anybody new who needs to learn the subtleties, that's where we do it. We prepare for upgrades in there too, and share good practice. They really are high powered meetings." The main thing, as the manager we cite above says, is "learning the processes."

Learning how to master enterprise systems: the "how" factor

The implementation of an ES in an organization typically follows a progressive approach based on the gradual adoption of the system throughout the enterprise. The primary goal should be to establish social networks through which the implementation and subsequent diffusion is guided. This implies taking a long-term perspective, instead of short/mid-term. Organizations should place far-less emphasis on the time span of projects. Projects will be created, utilized and sometimes discarded as part of a long-term journey led by key users. There is nothing wrong with the latter case. Projects can be discarded. This is not the same thing as failure. Project failure does not happen when the social networks are still healthy and learning is ongoing. The role of vendors and top managers should be to create the appropriate organizational conditions for encouraging learning and sharing mastery techniques within the different business areas.

Quoting a consultant from the most longstanding study:

> Organizations must take into account that there is a natural rejection of ES by companies not unlike that of transplanted organ. When a surgeon does an organ transplant one can only say it has been a success when the body accepts the new organ and the adaptation process occurs without a rejection. Putting the new organ into the body is just the beginning of the adaptation process. Using this metaphor for the ES phenomenon, the adaptation process of the new system (i.e. the new organ) would not occur until after the system is up and running; that is, when the key-users and users interact with the system. This means that modifications, improvements, new training,

etc. may then be required. The problem is that organizations invest a significant amount of money and resources for the implementation of a new system, but once it is up and running the key users are sent back to their previous positions, rather than being assigned a role in ensuring the use and diffusion of the ES throughout the organization.

This gradual adoption goes through phases that correspond to our three "what" factors: osmosis, growth and adaptation. Different roles should be assumed by different players. Key users, that is, those who develop most expertise and are formally or informally recognized by their colleagues as project leaders, should be placed in charge of the "what" factors. Senior managers can set the conditions for this journey and monitor its progress. Finally, the Chief Information Officer (CIO), IS specialists, and process consultants should give permanent support to key users and senior managers. Figure 4.1 describes the different roles to be assumed by these players to negotiate this long-term journey.

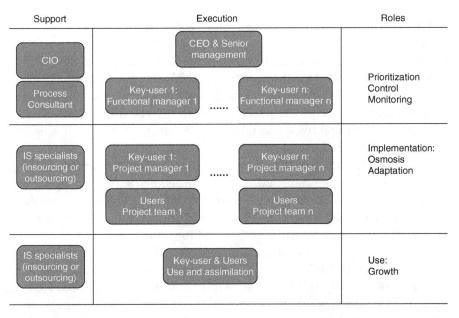

Figure 4.1 Long-term ES roles

Key users as the cornerstone of the journey to mastery

The term "key user" is native both to the companies studied in our investigation and to other ES and IS environments.[2] It relates to users of the system who play a designated role in implementing the system and helping other users learn about the system. The key users in this investigation were, for the most part, business-area managers, and their role were beyond the implementation project. We found that in most cases key users were playing further roles and activities related the development of three vital points: osmosis, growth and adaptation (see Figure 4.2). These roles and activities can be referred as the key behaviors for the biological evolution of an ES within a company.

Behavior can be defined as "a complex of observable and potentially measurable activities including motor, cognitive, and physiological classes of responses."[3] Behaviors should be described according to the intended goals they aim to achieve. From a deep analysis of the empirical data in our study, along with a review of ES and innovation literature,[4] we have defined six behaviors that influence the biological evolution of an ES throughout business areas: routine use, ongoing learning, user development, identification of mismatches, identification of new opportunities and project deployment.

In addition, we found a set of factors influencing key user behavior related to the ES evolution. Then, we have organized them according to a two-fold classification: environmental factors and individual factors. Environmental factors are those organizational stimuli that may influence the key users' behavior. We found the following four environmental stimuli functioning in reciprocal interaction with the key user behaviors: top managers' beliefs and roles, formal social networks, ES technical support, and internal help desk (see Figure 4.2).

Individual factors are related to cognitive factors, the models people hold, and how they are applied. "Cognitive factors partly dictate which external events will be observed, how they will be perceived, whether they leave any lasting effects, what valence and efficacy they have, and the information they convey will be organized for future use."[5]

In this investigation we have identified differences in key users' values, goals and ways of thinking that are significant in their effect on the performance of the ES evolution. It is akin to a biological evolution. Hence, we found that the following five personal factors functioned in a reciprocal interaction with key user behavior: thought patterns, self-efficacy, self-regulatory mechanisms, goals and prior knowledge (see Figure 4.2).

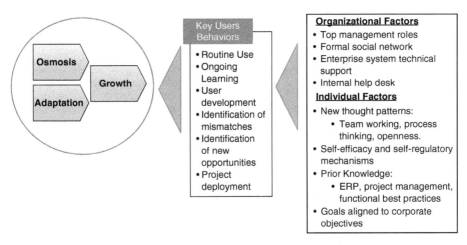

Figure 4.2 Key user behaviors influencing the biological evolution of an ES

Key user roles and behaviors

As mentioned earlier, we have defined six behaviors that influence the biological evolution of an ES throughout business areas. The six behaviors are described in the following subsections.

Routine use

This behavior refers to the use of the system as normal activity. This is the logical outcome of an ES adoption, but our experience shows that in a number of companies the ES is underused because users do not have the knowledge or the willingness to take full advantage of the system. We have classified routine use according to the six capabilities already presented through the concept of growth (see Box 3.2). They are as follows: (1) use of the system for the automation of business transactions, (2) use for decision-making support, (3) use for monitoring performance, (4) use for coordination, (5) use for customer service, and (6) use for the automation of process management. Hence, routine use as an "observable activity" implies taking advantage of different levels of capabilities from the ES.

By analyzing the routine use behavior of different key users in our investigation, we found distinct levels of ES utilization. For example, a key user in a sales and distribution area achieved the development of sophisticated ES functionality. Then, after rolling out the ES into the 12 sales

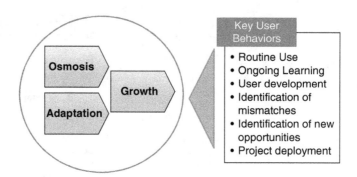

Figure 4.3 Key user behaviors influencing the biological evolution of an ES

regions (see Box 3.1), other end users started using the system to deliver a better customer service and to improve the coordination throughout the value chain.

One example provides a clear illustration of this benefit. Before the introduction of the ES, distribution intermediaries needed an average of four-hours (half-day) to acquire and load products onto their trucks in the company's sales transactions. After the process improvements took effect, the intermediaries only needed thirty minutes for the same sales transaction. This meant that they could pick up products twice a week instead of once a week. This reduced the intermediaries' average inventory by half and allowed them to use a vehicle of smaller capacity (reducing the cost of carrying inventory). These customer service improvements were widely appreciated by intermediaries. Then, the company planned to implement Business-to-Business (B2B) functionality for the sales process applied to large clients. Large supermarkets and chains would be able to send electronic sales orders to the company. By doing this, clients can order more easily and speedily than ever before. That would be translated into a higher customer service level, which is likely to allow the company to differentiate itself from competitors.

Ongoing Learning

As suggested by many experts, building proper behavior implies learning.[6] Learning as a behavior is related to two types of learning: learning by doing and learning by observation.[7]

Organizations absorb new complex technology through learning by doing.[8] End users spend several years developing and understanding the strengths and weaknesses of the technology. Thereby, learning by doing is not the result of knowledge transfer from the originator to the user of the technology. The point is the opposite: the need for learning and skill formation is in situ, far from the originator. A key user in a logistics area recognized that he learned about ES functionality and features by using it. As he mentioned, "this was like learning using videogames at home; this was a trial and error process."

A critical factor supporting the ES journey is learning by observation. "By observing others, one forms rules of behavior, and on future occasions this coded information serves as a guide for action."[9] Modeling procedures are effective for reducing excessive fears and facilitating the development of new patterns of behavior. A key user in a purchasing area showed the best evidence of learning by observation. Even though he was initially reluctant to use the system, after his first participation in key user meetings, he started a learning process based on his observation of how other key users were taking advantages from the ES. For example, he learnt about how the service functionality could help him to have better communication with the information technology department.

User development

Given that the ES implementation is in this way a continuous process, final user development also is an ongoing "observable activity." Key users support the development of his/her final users through three types of activities: (1) training, (2) guidance and (3) problem solving.[10]

In our investigation, training was mainly developed by ES consultants and/or organizational change agents. Guidance was given by key users to end-users by sending clear messages and guidelines about how the system should work. In the most successful cases, there was an emphasis on quickly solving problems related to the use of the system. This could be delivered through a help desk at first level and then by the ES consultants in the back-office. This overall user development activity could give rise to the writing of users' manuals and procedures. Taken together, all these activities can be considered as a knowledge transfer process to end users. The logistics key user described his role with a clear idea of his responsibility: "key users must send down the knowledge and information to the end users."

Identification of mismatches

The routine use of the ES could give rise to the identification of mismatches between the real business processes and the modeled business processes within the ES.[11] This kind of mismatch can have many causes. It might, for example, relate to organizational needs not considered previously in the analysis activity; or this mismatch might "appear" as key-users understand the true ramifications of the ES integration concept after they have gained some use of the system.[12]

The identification of mismatches is an "observable activity" that we found in the analysis of key users' behaviors. One of the remarkable examples of mismatch in one of the companies under study was that related to the procurement of indirect materials. The mismatch here emerged because the ES had initially been tailored to follow the way the company was already performing this process. First, the company tailored the system to support a requisition for material (RFM) from departments to the central warehouse. This was not in the system's standard functionality. Second, this RFM was printed to follow an approval chain. This worked for goods supplied internally. However, if the required material was not available in the central warehouse, the printout of the RFM was then sent to the procurement department to create a purchase order to the respective supplier. This involved the re-entry in the system of the data previously used to create the RFM. As the reader can deduce, this initial solution did not exploit the potential for ES to integrate effectively. Over time, key users understood the ES integration philosophy. It followed that a more integrated business model was developed and configured in the system.

Identification of new opportunities

The use of the system could give rise to the identification of new opportunities. These opportunities refer to the implementation of new functionality or the rollout of the functionality to other regions or locations.[13] The identification of new opportunities is an "observable activity." In all cases under study, we found that the ES journey followed an iterative and virtuous process of identifying and implementing further functionality. As one senior manager argued, "the ES objectives moved in the degree in which our needs were satisfied; first was the automation of our processes, then the subsequent frontier became to use the system for realizing the measurement and control of performance indicators." The logistics key user already mentioned found the opportunity to implement the Distribution Requirement Planning (DRP) technique throughout the distribution processes after the system was up and running the transactional activities. He recognized that he did not know anything about the DRP technique and the ES allowed him to learn and identify this best practice.

Project deployment

Once a key user identifies a mismatch or a new opportunity, a new project can be deployed. The project deployment is an observable activity that implies project planning, project implementation and project closing along with the ES technical support.[14] Seen as part of the longer Long Conversation, projects again become tactical stimuli, designed to achieve fixed goals and maybe succeeding. They are, of course, very relevant for the implementation and execution of the ES evolution.

Key users play the role of sponsors of their projects, and they have to convince key stakeholders (e.g., other key users and top management) and plan the project. Once the project is approved and planned, key users play the role of leaders of their initiatives. They implement and close the project along with the final, end users and the ES technical support. There are several examples of key users using project management techniques (e.g., Gantt, project control and monitoring) to successfully perform their ES projects.

Organizational and individual factors

Theorists argue that people behavior is influenced by two types of stimuli: environmental factors and individual factors.[15] As mentioned, we found a set of factors influencing key user behavior related to the ES evolution (Figure 4.4).

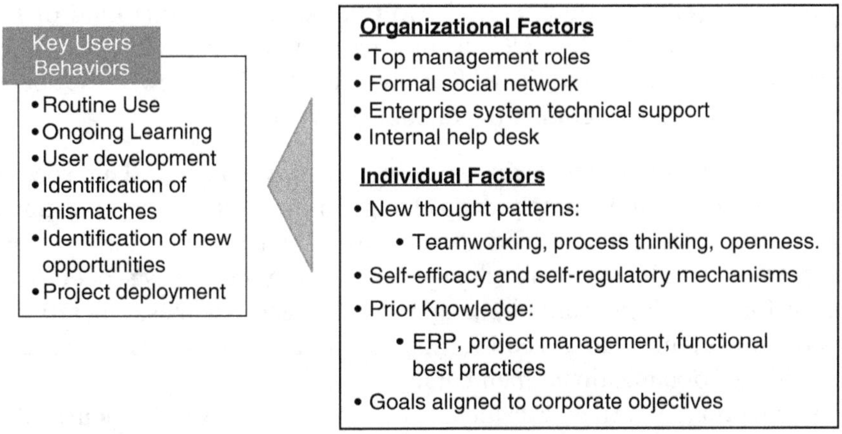

Key Users Behaviors

- Routine Use
- Ongoing Learning
- User development
- Identification of mismatches
- Identification of new opportunities
- Project deployment

Organizational Factors

- Top management roles
- Formal social network
- Enterprise system technical support
- Internal help desk

Individual Factors

- New thought patterns:
  - Teamworking, process thinking, openness.
- Self-efficacy and self-regulatory mechanisms
- Prior Knowledge:
  - ERP, project management, functional best practices
- Goals aligned to corporate objectives

Figure 4.4 Organizational and individual factors

Organizational factors

Top managers' beliefs and roles   In all our cases, the ES was formally led by top managers, including the CEO in some specific situations. Their beliefs about the importance of implementation activities in order to take full advantage of the system were critical in the evolution of the ES journey. These beliefs drove them to lead and closely manage implementation activities. Thus, they continuously played two roles: prioritizing and monitoring projects. Prioritizing refers to making the decision of what project initiatives should be performed first. This prioritization translated into resource allocation. Monitoring refers to controlling the performance of the ES and its biological-type evolution. This resulted in actions that kept the process on track.

In one of the cases, the CEO and senior managers often participated in key users meetings. They dedicated a part of this participation to monitoring the progress of each project. As mentioned by one of the key users: "the CEO was always behind us, like a shadow." The CEO and senior managers also asked to continuously raise the standards and to achieve better performance. For example, they pressed key users on month-end financial closing: "We should perform the logistics and financial monthly closing more efficiently. I am really worried. We are working until twelve midnight on the closing day to finish the work. We have to finish by six p.m."[16]

Formal social networks   In a number of cases, and normally based on the recommendation from ES consultants, top managers created specific committees composed of key users. We called them Key User Committees (KUC), which played two critical roles for this kind of ES biological evolution: (1) KUC as the environment whereby key users learnt by observation, and (2) KUC as the catalyst that allowed the social network to work, accelerating the biological evolution.

KUC as the environment for learning by observation   The special characteristics of an ES imply deep change in the adopting organizations. Its sheer scale, standardized functionality, integration and process perspective entails enormous changes in the way company's operations are performed. Even more challenging is the fact that these operational and organizational changes call for the modification of beliefs, values and behaviors of organizational members.[17]

As mentioned earlier, a critical factor supporting the ES journey is learning by observation. In our investigation, KUC became the perfect environment in which key users modeled new ways of thinking and behaviors from top managers and other organizational members. In the KUC meetings, many dialogues between top managers and the key users were influenced by different messages, patterns of thought, behavior rules and judgmental standards. These interactions were important for supporting the ongoing changes. One of these messages was that of business integration and team-work. For one of the CEOs, achieving the benefits of an ES relied increasingly on working in teams for the design of the new process, and less on a paradigm of individual work. A second message delivered by other top manager was that of knowledge sharing. In order for a system like an ES to work, it is vital to share data, information, and knowledge openly.

In one of the cases, the CEO took the decision to reduce the power of one of the key users within his broad business area (the whole supply chain) because of his perceived reluctance to change his behavior. Instead, three new key users were assigned to take charge of manufacturing, transportation and purchasing respectively. Hence, the other key users witnessed the consequences of not adapting to the demands of the project as interpreted by top managers. Much social learning is fostered by observing the actual performance of others and the consequences for them.[18]

The KUC created an environment wherein key users learnt by observation to promote new behaviors among the members of their business areas. For example, some key users often organized short meetings with their own staff to find answers to mismatches between processes and systems when they were found by someone in the department. The solutions then agreed were passed to the formal ES support function to develop a technical solution.

Finally, the KUC was an environment that reduced key users' fears and inhibitions. This was more visible with new key users (e.g., the above-stated transportation and manufacturing key users). Although they were initially quiet during the KUC meeting, they paid attention to the topics discussed by the rest of the members.

The different dynamics evolving from the KUC meetings gave rise to a set of judgmental and evaluative standards modeled by those judged to be the "best" key users in this social network. Stipulations were made on how members of this committee behaved:

> Everyone has to come to this meeting with clear information about what is happening in their areas, commented the CEO.
> Key users have to meet with their final users before coming here, commented one of the key users.

KUC as the catalyst that allowed the social network to work   Formal social networks are new forms of organizational design that promote the horizontal networking across the company. Formal networks allow

---

Box 4.1   Formal network in the Coffee Company: dialogue in a Key Users Committee meeting between the manufacturing key user, an ES consultant, and the company's CEO, while solving some system incidences in the area

ES Consultant: We are now checking the users' roles within the system. One of them which raise doubts is that of approving changes in the coffee formula for a particular production batch.

L&M Key User: I must be the only one approving changes in the coffee formula.

CEO: Well, even though you were the only one approving those changes, it would be better if the production supervisor learnt how to do them.

ES Consultant: But, the problem was that at a certain moment the blend was changed during the production process and before closing that specific batch.

Finance Key User: If this happened, the production cost for that batch is not real. We should sit down together and agree how to do this kind of thing. We should define a clear procedure for this. I do not care how you (L&M key users) do that, but it is critical to know when you do that and that everything is transparent for the financial area.

ES Consultant: Well, if you don't mind, let's have a meeting to discuss and define a procedure and roles to define and change a blend of coffee.

This example shows how four key actors exchanged information and influenced one another in a decision for defining a procedure in a particular fine-tuning of the system. The important issue here is that it is bad practice to change coffee blends during the production process. This was revealed during this conversation. As a result of the opportunity to exchange different points of view in an integrated meeting (that of the KUC), a new and more integrated perspective was defined to refine the process and the system.

organizations to enable collaborative work. Several studies and authors reinforce the role of formal social networks for the development of new behaviors and the development of a culture of knowledge sharing and collaboration.[19]

The KUC functioned as the catalyst that allowed the social network to precipitate this kind of ES biological evolution. These committees played a key role as the hub of a social network in which key users shared information, gave meaning to the information they exchanged, gained understanding of each other's views, and influenced each other.[20]

In Box 4.1, we describe one example of how the formal network functioned as a catalyst in the Coffee Company.[21] The formal network allowed for the exchange of different points of view in an integrated way. Then, new and more integrated perspectives were often defined, giving rise to the refinement of processes and the system.

ES technical support Although formal social networks serve a functional purpose and business committees maintain responsibility for the overall ES evolution, technical support from ES experts remains important. In some cases, this technical support was developed as an internal capability but in others, firms preferred to hire ES external consultants.

In one of the cases, the pattern of ES evolution was developed by key users along with an ES outsourcer. There were three motivations behind the adoption of ES outsourcing: (1) personnel turnover, (2) costs, and (3) facilitating change. In a previous experience, this company lost several internal people participating in the initial implementation; they took their knowledge away with them. In addition, paying external consultants in a traditional way was too expensive for a mid-size company. Therefore, the company decided to explore different models of supporting the ES journey. ES outsourcing was appealing in this light. Having a fixed price for everything was seen as a positive stimulus for the ES ongoing process. Without economic limitations, the ES journey relied on the key users and top managers' ability to define and implement new initiatives.

In another case, a large company preferred to develop a center of excellence composed of hundreds of internal consultants implementing and diffusing the ES throughout the company in all Europe. The ES was seen as a strategic weapon for the improvement of their processes and as a consequence the system support was seen as a critical internal capability.

Internal help desk A number of help desks were set-up for specific functionality and organizational areas in many cases. Consistently, the idea was to encourage users to ask questions and uncover doubts related to a recent implementation in specific areas. This was a means of knowledge transfer and allowed guidance to be given to final users. In addition, analysis of these questions allowed key users to know what new training should be developed or if the system required fine-tuning.

Individual factors

Thought patterns: A thought pattern is a certain way of thinking about our experiences and it is able to guide our judgments and actions in future events.[22] In this study, we have identified three ways of thinking influencing what we term as an "ES biological evolution." These ways of thinking have been coded as dyads of opposite patterns. They are described as follows:

Individual versus team working patterns: This dyad refers to how a person prefers to do a specific activity. We have found that a team-working pattern has a positive influence on behavior with regard to achieving ES deployment. The involvement of end users, knowledge sharing with others, and the joint-work with ES consultants were observed patterns in successful key users. However, we also found some key users representing the other extreme of working: that of working as an individual. It seems that these key users were very happy making individual decisions and sharing them with as small a number of people as possible. In fact, their end users were almost isolated from this process of ES biological evolution.

Process versus functional patterns: This dyad refers to how an individual understands, models and undertakes the set of activities he or she carries out in the organization. A process pattern means the person sees his or her activities as part of a whole that requires coordination with others. A functional pattern means that the person understands these activities as being isolated from the rest of the activities and that coordination with others is not needed. Successful key users showed a process pattern of thinking. They designed the processes and configured the system under a broad perspective of coordination and integration. On the contrary, however, we also saw that other key users based their actions on a functional pattern of thinking. Their narrower perspective conditioned them to argue that their business areas did not require coordination with others and the system would register only some transactions needed by others.

Openness versus closeness patterns: This dyad refers to the level of open-minded thinking a person has to new ideas or challenges. These two ways of thinking are also known as "opportunity thinking" and "obstacle thinking."[23] Opportunity thinking focuses on constructive ways of thinking with challenging situations. Obstacle thinking is the reverse. Opportunity thinking was observed in successful key users, whose were always searching for new ideas and practices embedded within the system, a very open-minded attitude. On the contrary, other key users exhibited obstacle thinking, until the point he preferred being substituted by others, then again, changing his/her mind.

Self-efficacy Self-efficacy is a significant concept in the area of psychology, and this has been used in a number of studies to explain the influence of individual factors on behavior. Self-efficacy can be defined as the "judgment of one's capability to accomplish a certain level of performance."[24]

   In our study, we found some evidence that the key user's self-efficacy in dealing with the ES biological evolution (i.e., osmosis, growth and adaptation) was a key element affecting the ES journey. From this perspective, we can talk about ES self-efficacy as potentially a judgment of a key user's capability to deploy an ES in his/her business area. Some evidence suggests that successful key users have the capability to be in charge of mastering the system throughout their business areas, promoting the use of the system by final-users, and using the system for their own benefit.

Self-regulatory mechanisms   There is also evidence that successful key users set standards of behavior for themselves and respond to their own actions with self-reward or self-punishment. Self-regulation of behavior can be described as composed of three different components: (1) an evaluative dimension, (2) a judgmental function and (3) a self-evaluative reaction.[25] The evaluative dimension represents the performance measure. In this study, we observed "perceptual quality" as one of the measures adopted by successful key users. This measure is normally used for achievement-oriented activities. The judgmental function is defined by personal standards and/or a social referent. In this study, the social referent was often based on the standard norms driven by the formal social networks. Key users often evaluated themselves according to a collective comparison, producing rewardable or punishable consequences.

Goals Goals have strong motivational effects and successful key users showed clear and challenging goals. When the previously mentioned logistics key user identified the opportunity for implementing a Distribution Resource Planning (DRP) technique, he stated a clear objective for this undertake based on the integration of downstream processes through a planning process. He also knew this was a challenging goal, even more when one considers this new technique implied new knowledge for final users and higher levels of integration. Finally, proximity was fundamental for success. In other words, the key user stated proximal goals, phase by phase, to ensure motivation and achievement throughout their end users. In our study, some key users' goals played a role as motivator, and in other cases there was a lack of clear and proximal goals.

Prior Knowledge   Individual skills also play a critical role for the ES biological evolution. Success requires skills and self-efficacy. We found two different types of skills influencing the ES journey. The skills were related to key users' prior knowledge of specific competencies. When an organization's members possess greater prior knowledge, they can absorb new knowledge more effectively.[26] Consequently, the organizational members (e.g., key users) can internalize and exploit that knowledge for the benefit of his/her business area.[27] The key user's prior knowledge coded is therefore as follows:

Prior knowledge of ES   This concept refers to the key user's prior knowledge about ES implementation and use. Those key users with a prior knowledge of ES were better equipped to master the use of the system more effectively.

Project management skills   This is the prior knowledge of key users on the topic of project management. Project management skills remained key to the longer ES Long Conversation. Project management skills involved the use of knowledge to schedule, implement and monitor activities to ensure that the project goals were achieved.

How it worked in one case

The Coffee Company provides a useful example of how mastering an ES works. There, the formal social networks focused on the key-user committee (KUC). Initially, the committee had the normal terms of reference of other implementations, but it became the focus of a social network over time. The stakeholders in the committee sought to ensure the assimilation, diffusion and improvement of the ES. The evolution of KUC to this role was gradual. Users were responsible for creating and sharing knowledge related to the ES transformation. In this, nodes of expertise emerged; some users took on key roles and began to lead the development of appropriate attitudes toward the mastery of the system within their areas.

In addition, the CEO and senior managers were continuously participating in the KUC. This resonates with evidence of other cases in the latter stages of their projects. Our evidence shows how the company's CEO continuously reinforced new patterns of behavior such as using the system, coaching other users, requesting the diffusion of the system to new areas, taking advantage of the system functionality, and continuously and openly thinking of how to improve processes.

Finally, the support role from CIO, ES specialists and consultants was crucial for the technical development and adaptation of the system. Although users took over the ownership of the ES, they needed technical support to address their functional and business initiatives. Hence, these users could balance their ES development with their daily activities. The Coffee Company outsourced ES technical support.

Coffee Company's sales and distribution area

The Coffee Company's sales and distribution area (S&D) was responsible for the processes of sales and delivery from regional centers to retailers. The area had a manager who was also designated as the key user for the evolution of the ES within his area.

To understand how the three factors (i.e., key user behavior, individual factors and organizational factors) influenced the biological evolution of the ES work within the sales and distribution area, we describe in the following text how the behavior of the sales and distribution key user evolved during three and half years to achieve his goal of mastering the system throughout his business area. It is argued in this description that

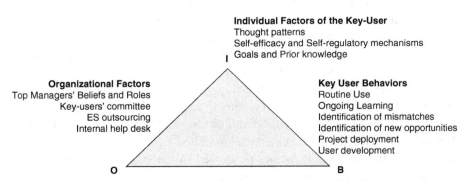

Figure 4.5 Factors influencing the mastering of ES within the Coffee Company

his behavior (B) was influenced by individual factors (I) and the organizational environment (O). This description is based on the social learning theory and represented through triads of B-I-O (i.e., behavior, individual factor and organizational factor).[28] Figure 4.5 depicts the triad. Figures 4.6 and 4.7 describe the way this mastering works for the specific case of the sales and distribution area in the Coffee Company.

In year 2 of our study, the S&D functionality was already installed in the factory and diffusion started throughout the rest of the remote regions of the country. The project initiation (B) was the first "observable activity" performed by the key user (see triad 1 in Figure 4.6). This activity was initially planned to be undertaken in one of the regional distribution centers. This would be the pilot diffusion project. This project initiation (B) was positively influenced by the CEO's beliefs and roles (O). The CEO had previously suggested in a KU meeting that the sales and distribution processes were a priority for the ES journey. This decision was mainly influenced by the industrial environment. Competition and demanding customers (e.g., large retailers) were pushing toward "excellence." Moreover, the CEO continuously asked in the KUC for more and better figures of sales in remote regions. Real time information was critical for facing the competition and meeting clients' needs.

The individual factors (I) of the key user determined that the environmental events were relevant and compatible with his own goals. This key user had the clear and proximal goal of standardizing the processes of his 12 regional centers. He had suffered the organizational chaos of managing twelve silos for many years. His views were moulded by that. He espoused the benefits of managing a business from a process perspective (instead of functionally). According to his way of thinking, a continuous improvement pattern required him to initiate and execute this project. His previous ES experience in another food company had enhanced his self-efficacy in tackling this kind of project. He was also convinced of the usefulness of this system to improve the company's processes and had a clear knowledge of the area's needs. In short, both the organizational and individual factors positively influenced his attitude toward the initiation and execution of this project.

During the same year 2 of our study, the S&D functionality was successfully implemented in the first remote regional center (see triad 2 in Figure 4.6). The project execution and closing (B) was undertaken by the key user and two change agents were assigned by the KU committee. In addition to the individual factors described in the triad 1, we found that this key user had previous experience and knowledge of project management (I).

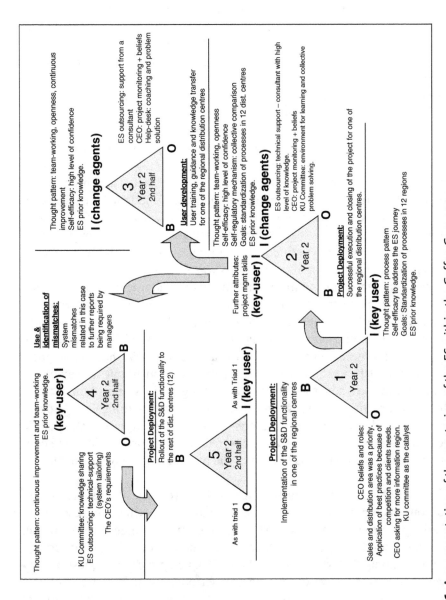

Figure 4.6 A representation of the mastering of the ES within the Coffee Company

In the case of the two change agents, their individual and cognitive factors were positive components of this triad. We would like to mention in particular the following: team-working and openness, prior experience using enterprise systems and high levels of confidence to tackle this process (i.e., self-efficacy), and a high standard of behavior appreciated by others. Attitudes toward team-working and openness were critical aspects of embarking on this journey. Change agents were always receptive to opinions from others who would be the final-users in remote regions. This gave rise to an open and confident environment for change where they gradually gained respect from others. The successive successes in subsequent regions then created a "friendly reception" environment elsewhere. Reciprocally, their performance (B) strengthened their self-efficacy (I) and enhanced the favorable environment for change (O). Moreover, the members of the KU committee had their eyes on the project. Their high expectations helped raise the performance standards of the team (i.e., key user and change agents). The team was embedded in what is called a "social comparison" context. This gave rise to a self-regulatory process in which the change agents were continuously working on the search for excellence in the project. They recognized that this was stressful.

The organizational environment was also fundamental for the good performance (B) of this team. Three aspects were relevant: ES technical support, the CEO's project monitoring role, and the KU committee as a catalyst. The change agents held the role placed by the ES outsourcing in high esteem. One of them described it as follows: "We had the support of a consultant from the outsourcing firm. This consultant was available for everything whenever we needed something. This is important because when you are implementing and using a system anything can happen. Once we needed to ring her (the consultant) late at night to ask specific questions about certain problems we were unable to sort out. She (the consultant) came and helped us to resolve the problem. She gave us invaluable help."

The CEO was constantly monitoring the progress of this project. In addition to keeping an eye on project variables (e.g., time and resources), he also gave the regions support for change management. For example, he would phone a regional manager in a remote center unannounced. He would ask about different aspects of the diffusion project and question why certain sales figures were not reaching set objectives. This was possible because the CEO now had real-time information relating to all regional centers. The unexpected call received by the regional manager in turn gave rise to a feeling of "this is important for the boss." Thus, the CEO was encouraging new types of behavior.

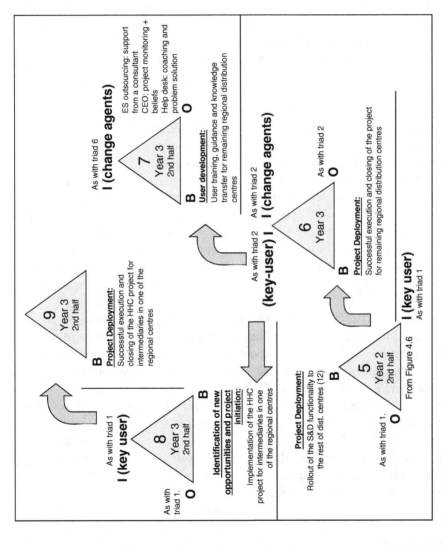

Figure 4.7 A representation of the mastering of the ES within the Coffee Company

The closing of the project in the pilot regional center automatically triggered the next action (B): user development (see triad 3 in Figure 4.6). As mentioned earlier, final user development was not just a question of training. The change agents were coaching, guiding and transferring knowledge to final users (B). After the system was up and running in the first regional center, the change agents (I) and the designated ES consultant (O) were in place for two weeks, stabilizing the system and solving any problem that arose. This was a learning process (B) for the center final users. After these two weeks, an internal help desk (O) took the role of giving remote support to final users. The two change agents were part of this help desk. They recognized that most inquiries coming from the regional centers were related to procedures and norms, rather than system issues. Additional training (B) was planned to bridge the identified gaps.

In parallel to observable user development activity (B), the use and identification of mismatches (B) occurred (see triad 4 in Figure 4.6). This activity was mainly developed by the key user who was in charge of the evaluation of the daily activities. As a member of the KU committee, he also shared knowledge with the others and received additional requirements from the CEO and senior managers (O). In particular, we can mention the identification of mismatches (B) related to new reports required by senior management. These requirements activated the system tailoring carried out by the ES outsourcer (O). A continuous improvement mind-set (I) encouraged identification of mismatches (B) and the definition of new requirements (B).

Finally, the triad 5 in Figure 4.6 represents the project initiation (B) of the rollout of the sales and distribution functionality to the remaining 11 regional centers. This was carried out on a one-by-one basis, but we have described all 12 projects as a single activity for the sake of brevity. As described in Figure 4.6, the I and O components in triads 5, 6 and 7 are similar to those in triads 1, 2 and 3. Triads 8, 9 and 10 in Figure 4.7 described the identification of the new opportunity related to hand-held computers for intermediaries, the project initiation of this new opportunity, and the project execution throughout the 12 S&D centers (B). The individual and organizational factors for this set of behaviors were similar to the previous diffusion activities described earlier.

Conclusions

Key points

- This ES journey is a Long Conversation in which attaining the mastery of the system becomes increasingly the central concern of the mission.

- This long-term journey is led by key users, who are responsible for the development of the evolution through a biological model of osmosis, growth and adaptation. Six behaviors or observable activities are critical for this development: routine use, ongoing learning, user development, identification of mismatches, identification of new opportunities and project deployment.
- The role of top managers (i.e., the CEO and senior managers) is to create the appropriate organizational conditions to encourage these key user behaviors through different business areas. A fundamental means to achieve this objective is the creation of formal social networks designed for the long-term and composed of the key users.
- Key users will be responsible for the development of these behaviors toward the mastery of the system within their business areas. Also, they are responsible for creating, sharing and diffusing the knowledge appropriated for this long-term journey.
- The mastery relies on individual and organizational factors. Prior knowledge and cognitive capabilities of key users and their team. The better-equipped would move faster, the less-equipped would go more slowly with a first goal of assimilating new skills, values and behaviors. This makes for a long journey to achieve the business goals related to the diffusion of an ES.

CHAPTER 5

Building organizational capabilities for the Long Conversation

We have argued that the implementation of enterprise systems (ES) in an organization should follow a progressive approach based on the gradual adoption of systems throughout the enterprise. Once a technological baseline is established, the primary goal should be to develop organizational capabilities through which the implementation and subsequent diffusion is guided.

In this chapter, we discuss the organizational capabilities required for the Long Conversation. We will show why osmosis, growth and adaptation require a different set of capabilities to the ones typically used during initial stages of ES adoption. To identify those capabilities, we explore the dominant paradigm of ES implementation and discover why it eventually hits a wall, losing traction and effectiveness. At that decisive moment, organizations reach a reflection stage, and if their managers want to keep advancing and materializing the business promises of ES, a change of paradigm becomes imperative. What is that new paradigm and how does it determine the organizational capabilities required to advance in the Long Conversation? As we show, it is more social than technical, more organic than mechanistic, more systemic than systematic, more concerned with uncertainty and effectiveness than certainty and efficiency.

The initial phase of ES adoption: expectations and results

At the risk of over-simplification, the "typical" context of ES adoption in the initial phase can be summarized as follows:

- The company is in pain because of legacy systems deficiencies in automation and coordination. Several key business rules are not supported by legacy systems and are therefore performed manually, creating an inflexible and unreliable work-system. Furthermore, on the coordination side, integrated processes try to flow across different organizational functions, facing diverse ill-integrated legacy systems, which results in defects and rework and increases interface costs and process cycle time.

- Enter the ES with the promise of solving the root causes of these organizational pains, creating business value from better internal and external (business system) integration, and providing flexibility to accommodate new business rules and processes.[1]
- Management objectives center first on minimizing pain from legacy systems and second on maximizing business value from the ES. However, Information Technology (IT) in general has a long history of non-realized potential, combined with typical cost and time overruns. The ES is a large IT system, and the adopting company is not particularly familiar with it. Hence, as a cautionary measure, management decides to subject their objectives to strong restrictions expressed as time and budget constraints.[2]

Table 5.1 Management approach typically used in the initial phase of ES adoption

Element	Description
Strategy	Identify areas of intervention: (1) notorious problem areas associated to legacy system deficiencies in automation and coordination, and (2) processes in the enterprise architecture with critical role in business strategy. Map these areas in the ES architecture, and identify candidate modules. Analyze the business case and select definite modules to be implemented.
Leadership	CEO sponsors ES Adoption. Key user team is formed with high-level representatives of each area to be affected.
People	Specialists from the business unit to be affected and their corresponding support areas (technology and process), with deep knowledge of current process and how they are executed with the current IT applications. Internal and/or external consultants in charge of planning and implementation.
Organizational Structure and Coordination	Hierarchy: authority flowing through top-down vertical lines to ensure alignment and compliance with intended objectives. Key user team: horizontal inter-unit team expected to provide an integrated perspective for ES adoption.
Planning and Control	ES adoption follows project management discipline, emphasizing sub-disciplines of project scope, time schedule, quality, cost and risk.[3] Sub-projects corresponding to different ES modules and organizational areas are cascaded and interconnected.
Motivation	Expectation of pain reduction from legacy systems serves as a common motivator. Potential for greater business value from the ES works as a secondary, less compelling and more uncertain motivator.
Change Management	Communication of project objectives is combined with strong persuasion from influential leaders (CEO and key users). Top-down hierarchical authority demands compliance. As an ultimate resource, stubborn resistance is usually fired.

As described in previous chapters, companies face this initial phase of ES adoption using the organizational cocktail depicted in Table 5.1.

Our case studies show that after pushing the ES into the organization following this approach, the typical results are as follows:

- Several ES modules are initially implemented, with some degree of customization.[4]
- Legacy systems are displaced and better automation is achieved through more flexible, more robust, business rules now contained into the ES. Also, some initial coordination (integration) is achieved. As a result, participants recognize (some degree of) satisfaction and leaders decree (some degree of) success.
- However, most people, both users and IT specialists, declare that the ES brought about its own dose of complexity in terms of use and maintenance.
- There is a feeling that the system is adding less value than it is capable of, in terms of vendors' promises and/or management initial claims of expected business value.
- Initial implementation has taken more time and resources than expected, and it has demanded a lot of effort. Projects were stretched, sometimes too much. In other cases, when budget was insufficient, project scope was downsized.
- Business and IT people have worked together side by side more intensively than in previous IT implementations. The ES team has achieved an interesting level of integration: business people are more sensible to IT issues and vice-versa.

How should these results be interpreted? We propose four success criteria, as illustrated in Table 5.2.

According to these criteria, which can be easily extrapolated to any other large IT system, an ES has been successfully adopted by a company when current pain associated to legacy system deficiencies have been overcome, the ES has created value by supporting the business strategy, the project plan has been executed without major time and cost overruns, and business and IT people have increased their mutual understanding of each other's world, which provides for a better win-win IT management capability.[5]

Going back to the results of our case studies, we could argue, as shown in Table 5.3, that the initial phase of IT adoption usually ends with a reasonable success in ES efficiency at the expense of ES effectiveness, apparent success in ES adoption process efficiency, compensated with some gains in ES adoption process effectiveness.

Table 5.2 Success criteria for ES adoption

	Enterprise System as a *Solution*	Enterprise System Adoption *Process*
Business and Organizational *Effectiveness*	Does the *ES* achieve expected *objectives* in terms of stakeholder's *value* (profitability, competitiveness, customer loyalty and supplier cooperation)?	Does the Adoption Process produce greater *integration* of business and technology inside the organization, i.e., a domain *maturity* that could be *leveraged in the future*?
Business and Organizational *Efficiency*	Have *inefficiencies* associated to previous legacy systems' automation and integration deficiencies been substantially reduced by the ES?	Has the organization been able to implement the ES in time and in budget, avoiding overruns and overspending that could deteriorate the ES business case?

Table 5.3 Typical success criteria for ES adoption – case studies

	Enterprise System as a Solution	Enterprise System Adoption Process
Business and Organizational Effectiveness	LOW ES has more potential than was achieved in initial phase of adoption.	MEDIUM Integration between business and IT domain improved somewhat, a maturity that could be leveraged in the future
Business and Organizational Efficiency	HIGH Significant reduction in automation inefficiencies of legacy systems (in selected areas of implementation)	MEDIUM-LOW Some cost and time overruns, and/or sacrifices in scope or business objectives to meet constraints.

The salient success of the initial phase of ES adoption in most cases is the significant reduction in the organizational pain caused by automation inefficiencies of legacy systems (of course, this is in those areas where ES modules were implemented). Strict project management is able to provide some degree of efficiency in the adoption process.[6] But, when time and cost constraints are reached, management reflects on the initial goal of maximizing the business value promise of ES, and it realizes that the project has fall short of expectations. Pain has been reduced but satisfaction has not been generated! Somehow disconcerted by the gap between expectations and results, management reflects on some unexpected gains. IT and business people have become closer by working together on the project. This mutual understanding of business and technological issues is new. And management wonders what to do. Figure 5.1 shows this reflection point.

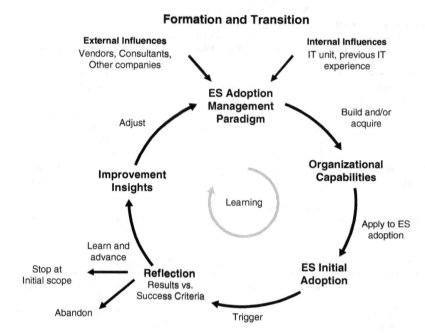

Figure 5.1 ES adoption management paradigm

   Our case studies show that the reflection point is like an epiphany that goes like this: "we did not get quite as much as we were expecting, but we can see the business value is there somewhere. This is tougher than we thought, but now business and IT people have learned to worked together, which is a nice sub-product of this effort that we were not expecting. If only we could leverage that and try further to create that business value we now see closer!"

Transition to the Long Conversation: a change of paradigm

What follows after the reflection point is fascinating. For the sake of sponsors and other key stakeholders, partial success is declared. At the same time, the organization is left to continue its slow path away from the glare of official project scrutiny. What happens next can only be described as a change of paradigm. A collective learning emerges from the initial projects: ES adoption is not about "inserting" a technology into an organization, it is more like transplanting an organ into an organism.

Transplants, as most surgical operations might be planned in detail, but what happens during the operation, and particularly after it, is a process of mutual adaptation between the organ and the organism. On one hand, part of the organism rejects the new organ creating and mobilizing antibodies against it. But, on the other hand, part of the organism accepts it, adapts to it and integrates it with other organs.

ES adoption is much like an organ transplant. It creates organizational resistance, and there is a natural reason for it: the organization is trying to preserve its current equilibrium, what system theorists, called homeostasis, a self-preservation property of any open system. But as ES usage broadens and deepens, its superior functionality triggers an acceptance response from the organization. Gradually, resistance fades and acceptance increases.

Two effects result from increased acceptance of ES into the organization: (1) management develops a sense of organizational success; the ES may not be a resonant business success yet, but having been able to transplant it effectively boosts management confidence for the future and (2) management realizes that its ES adoption has followed a "too technical" approach and that some organizational elements were lacking. The first effect helps explain why the companies in our case studies kept going with ES adoption into new uncharted territory: at that point, they became more confident that they could go beyond the initial project and look for that elusive ES business value. The second effect is a change of paradigm for ES adoption: from a mechanistic approach to an organic approach. This paradigm transition is critically important to understand the organizational capabilities required for Long Conversation. Thus, let us dig a little further into these paradigms.

The mechanistic approach, as the name suggests, considers the organization as a mechanism, that is, drawing analogies from the physical sciences, an organization is a set of entities and activities arranged to produce regularly, orderly, and predictably, a particular type of outcome. The mechanistic conception considers organizations as artifacts, whose purpose, structure and processes are designed from the outside.

In contrast, the organic approach, as the name suggests, considers the organization as an organism. This time, analogies are drawn from biology: an organization is subject to evolution, growth and development. It is a system (a whole) composed by a set of parts (subsystems) and interrelationships; more precisely, it is an open system, that responds to its environment, adapting if necessary to maintain homeostasis (equilibrium). Under the organic approach, organizations have some sort of internal intelligence (i.e., purpose, structure and processes may be generated from the inside).

The mechanistic approach is appropriate for handling structured complexity. By "structured complexity" we mean multidimensional situations in which many variables and their interactions have to be considered as part of the organizational transformation (complexity), but the key variables and their key interactions are well known before the transformation takes place (structured). As we mentioned earlier, the mechanistic approach considers organizations as artifacts, whose purpose, structure and processes are designed from the outside. Thus, adopting an ES under the mechanistic approach assumes that those in charge can perfectly determine the objectives, key organizational variables, and key organization interactions before the ES adoption starts and reflect all that perfect information in a plan. But, can they?

Figure 5.2 shows a model of organizations that considers some of their key dimensions: strategy, structure, technology, business processes, people and culture and management processes. Many such models can be proposed, but this one is simple enough to explain our argument.[7] When a business adopts an ES, this is a major change in the technological dimension. Adjustments have to be made in all other dimensions to integrate the ES into the organization. These mutual adjustments between dimensions are bidirectional. For example, we need to perform certain activities and processes to adopt the ES, and at the same time, the ES will transform the way business processes are performed. This, in turn, will affect organizational structure, but at the same time some structural elements (units, roles and teams) have to be put in place to conduct ES adoption. The ES is initially implemented to support certain strategic objectives, but after successful implementation, new potential capabilities of the ES are better understood, which can be oriented strategically to improve competitiveness. We can go on with the examples involving other dimensions such as people, their competences and behaviors (including acceptance and rejection of the ES), planning and control systems, incentives, and so on. But you get our point: the adoption of an ES (as well any other large IT system) will have an impact of multiple dimensions of any organization. And those impacts are bidirectional, including actions and reactions. Moreover, cause and effect ripple chains across all organizational dimensions occur as part of the adoption of an ES.

The situation we have just described is indeed quite complex, but it is not "structured." Management may wish to know the key variables in each organizational dimension to be affected by the ES, the reactions the ES will receive, and all the cause-effects chains that will be triggered across organizational dimensions. Unfortunately, that is wishful thinking. Management is really facing "unstructured complexity."

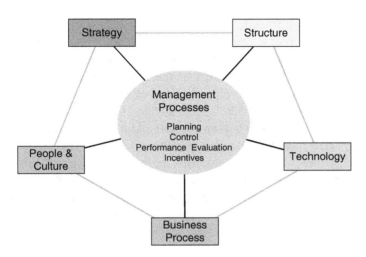

Figure 5.2 A multidimensional model of organizations

When the management approach, described in Table 5.1, conceived to handle a transformation characterized by "structured complexity" faces a significant degree of "unstructured complexity," a mismatch appears between the situation and the approach. The results described in Table 5.3 are a natural consequence. Unanticipated events appear as the ES adoption progresses. Mutual adaptation between the ES and people skills and behaviors, processes and work-systems, structural configuration and strategic direction, occurs gradually as action-reaction loops and cause-effect chains are resolved. These uncertainties cannot be contemplated ex-ante by structured project planning and cannot be easily accommodated through top-down hierarchical change management. Of course, some success is achieved, but at the cost of time and budget overruns, reduction of business aspiration and some sparks in the relationship between business and IT people. The results described in Table 5.3 can be explained as a mismatch between the "unstructured complexity" of large ES adoption and the "structured complexity" implicit in the mechanistic approach typically used.[8]

The epiphany management has after the initial phase of ES adoption is now clearer: "we have pushed the ES into the organization, the new organ (ES) has been somewhat forcefully inserted; by reducing pain from legacy systems we have gained a certain degree of net acceptance (acceptance minus rejection); this favorable state could be leveraged if we want to attain the potential business value of the ES, but from now on we have to conduct the process like an organ transplant, we need that the organization multi-dimensionally [Figure 5.2] accepts the new system." This is an organic approach, because it understands homeostasis. Adopting successfully the ES is equivalent to transforming the organization from the actual current status to the new desired one, while in the process preserving dynamic equilibrium between all organizational elements described in Figure 5.2.

In a later section in this chapter, we will address the distinctive elements that summarize the organic management approach to ES adoption. They are critical if we want to successfully continue the Long Conversation. For the moment, let us just state that osmosis, growth and adaptation, as described in chapters 3 and 4, are three distinctive ways to manage the unstructured complexity of ES adoption. But, before delving into this at, it is important to understand why the mechanistic approach dominates the initial phase of ES adoption.

Tech waves and business-IT misalignment

In our case studies, we have noticed consistently how experienced managers feel disconcerted during the phase of paradigm transition. Of course, in general, the process of abandoning a paradigm and assuming a new one is always unsettling and confusing. But our curiosity comes from the fact that managers wonder how they did not proceed organically from the beginning. Many of them have accomplished large transformations in their organizations, including launching new product lines, entering new market segments and/or different countries; they have conducted postmerger integrations, and even complete strategic turnarounds. They have handled unstructured complexity before, most of the times intuitively. So they wonder, why they did not used their organic management repertoire in the case of ES adoption?

We think this can be explained by two factors: how technology waves "hit" organizations and the large "domain distance" between IT and business people in most companies.

Tech waves, as we heard in Chapter 1, derive from invention and innovation. As they sweep across business sectors, each organization tries to make conscious decisions about why, when, where, and how to adopt the new technology. This decision is at the core of a corporation's technology strategy. Of course, management tries to control the process of technology adoption. However, the more dramatic an innovation is, the more difficult it is to provide for a smooth technology adoption. As in the beach, when the tech wave is very high at the moment it hits the organization, it is difficult not to get walloped by it, or we might say, wallowed around. Some companies handle this risk by deliberately being a late-adopter, a strategy that might create its own business risk of being left behind.

For our purpose, it is convenient to separate IT waves in two parts: front and back. Consider the front-edge of the wave for an early adopter. At the supply side, an innovation is disseminated by the IT industry, accompanied by intense marketing and sales efforts that are aimed to communicate the potential business value of the new IT. Risks, both technological and organizational, are downplayed, while benefits are communicated enthusiastically (sometimes hyperbolically). At the demand side, early adopters are motivated by the possibility of early-mover advantages. Public declarations about the decision to adopt tend to emphasize expectations of fast materialization of great economic value. Thus, the demand and supply dynamics of the front edge of the IT wave creates a dominant theme: "searching for tech-driven economic value."[9]

As the wave penetrates the organization, it changes character. At the supply side, vendors' role evolve from marketing to expert support. Meanwhile, at the demand side, key users who know they will have to live with the ES, are busy making sure the ES and business processes are adequately matched. This creates a lot of pressure for IT personnel and consultants who have to work in ES customization, development of satellite applications, and/or adaptation of processes to ES functionality.

At the back edge of the wave, the ES modules are finally deployed. The technical issues that were so dominant in the front-edge of the wave move to the sides, and attention turns to handling the transition from the current work-system to a new one enabled by the ES. This is a huge change for a large number of people. They have to develop a new set of skills and behaviors, and they have to do it fast to go on with the day-to-day operations. Social issues that had been in the shadows, now take center-stage. The dominant theme during the back edge of the IT wave is "searching for stability and organizational acceptance of the ES."

Although the front edge of the IT wave is tech-driven, the back edge is social-driven. Actually, both technological and social issues are present at all points along the wave, but definitely, when the IT wave initially hits the organization, the emphasis is technological, morphing into social as the wave enters the organization. As the long tail of the IT wave keeps diffusing inside the organization, a more balanced socio-technical approach tends to appear, where both aspects are considered and managed together. The socio-technical model, where organizations are understood through bidirectional interactions of technical and social variables, mutually adapting and searching for equilibrium and joint optimization, is a key element of our approach for the Long Conversation.[10]

Going back to our question of why experienced managers rely on a mechanistic approach in the initial phase of ES adoption, we have found that one key explanation is that the front edge of the tech-wave, the one that hits the organization first, is driven by a "searching for tech-driven economic value" theme. There is another factor that compounds the effect of the first one: the large "domain distance" between IT and business people in most companies.

People in IT and business domains have quite different world-views, value systems, motivational drivers, languages and competences. Any silo-organization exhibits some degree of organizational distance among different units, but this is very significant between IT and business people in most corporations. For evidence, it suffices to notice how, for several decades, the challenge of aligning business and IT has been a constant topic in the business literature and a recurring top issue in senior management agenda.

How does the large "organizational distance" between business and IT operate at ES adoption? At the initial phase of ES implementation, business people are (justifiably) intimidated by the complexity of the new IT. Technological discussions, driven by ES vendors and IT internal professionals, dominate the initial conversation. Since the IT issues are not easily understandable by many business people, they "retreat" on those issues and concentrate on the "ends" instead of the "means." Profusion of IT jargon does not help otherwise. Instead of trying to bridge the organizational distance between business and IT domain, business people emphasize what they want to get: to reduce pain from legacy systems and create business value from the ES potential. The IT people are happy to concentrate on the means as opposed to the ends, because after all, those are the issues they know how to handle. IT consultants (both external and internal) are incorporated to connect the means (ES) with the ends (business objectives), and they attempt to do it from an engineering perspective. Notice how organizational distance reinforces the mantra of "searching for tech-driven (IT means) economic value (business ends)."

Although organic organizational and social issues are notably absent in the original intentions of the initial phase of ES adoption, an interesting by-product of that phase is how, as shown in Table 5.3, after struggling with inserting the ES into the organization, the ES steering committee improves its integration between the business and IT domains. Cross-understanding of IT potential and limitations, business value objectives and the socio-technical nature of organizations is in itself a distinctive organizational capability; a capability that can be leveraged to continue ES adoption under a more organic approach. Companies that have achieved this realization are ready for a Long Conversation, one that requires a new set of organizational capabilities.

A new set of organizational capabilities

Engaging in the Long Conversation requires putting in place an organic approach to ES adoption. An approach that enables management to handled

Table 5.4 Organizational capabilities for the Long Conversation

Element	Description
Strategy	Bidirectional alignment between business and ES strategy. Key automation, coordination and information support opportunities are identified by a discovery process that contains Osmosis, Growth and Adaptation. ES strategy is not only deliberate, but also emergent.
Leadership	CEO creates the appropriate environment for exploring opportunities and learning; this environment is neither directive nor laissez faire but "involved and developmental." ES management team stimulates convergence of the learning process.
People	Key users are catalysts of learning acting as pivots between the deep intra-area perspective in their business and functional domains and the broad inter-area perspective of internal and external business processes and systems. Process and IT specialists work under a "prototype" mindset.
Organizational Structure and Coordination	Teams and Social Open Networks combined to provide both depth of dimensional (function, product, market segment, channel) detail, and breadth of multi-dimensional perspective. Effective governance by the ES management team with participation of key users.
Planning and Control	Directed incrementalism: a management decision making approach that balances direction (expressed as vision and objectives) with incremental execution. Visions are translated into strategic options and put into practice through action-learning. Fast learning cycles eliminate non promising options and concentrate resources on most promising ones, progressively revealing appropriate transition paths. This approach is key to handle the inherent uncertainty and political context of the Long Conversation.
Motivation	People motivated by an environment of collaboration, discovery, conjoint design and public recognition of contribution, combined with the satisfaction that results from achieving business value from ES by co-creating a path of small, progressive victories.
Change Management	Organizational and political gestation of the appropriate environment for the Long Conversation, centered on building awareness, credibility and pockets of commitment. Twofold emphasis along the journey on building both political support and capabilities for flexible discovery and experimentation.

"unstructured complexity" demands a different set of organizational capabilities, as summarized in Table 5.4. As we describe each capability, please
take some time to contrast it with the corresponding version in Table 5.1,
where the typical management approach used in the initial phase of ES
adoption was presented.

Strategy

At the initial phase of ES adoption, alignment with business strategy is
twofold: improve efficiency and control by eliminating automation and
coordination deficiencies from legacy systems, and support key processes
in the enterprise architecture with a critical role in business strategy.[11]
Most of the time, this approach looks at the ES as an enabler of the current strategy. This is clearly a desirable form of alignment, but it is unidi-
rectional. What about using the ES to create new strategic opportunities,
those that are not explicitly identified in the dominant strategic paradigm?
We are talking about complementing the deliberate ES strategy with emergent components: the latter ones cannot be identified before ES adoption
because they result from discovering opportunities through creativity and
learning in an uncertain business and organizational context.[12]

The Long Conversation proposes that well-known ES business benefits,
as explained by vendors, consultants and scholars are concepts, useful
abstractions that enable communication. They represent potential opportunities. But, the concrete opportunities available to a company depend
on its specific context. The processes of osmosis, growth and adaptation
described in chapters 3 and 4 are indeed discovery and learning processes
that connect potentiality with reality, desirability with feasibility, and concept with context. Through these three processes, key automation, coordination and information support opportunities are discovered. Some of
those opportunities will confirm the initial deliberate intention for the ES.
In other cases, new strategic possibilities will emerge. Through osmosis,
growth and adaptation, the ES strategy is crafted in a complex and uncertain environment.

Some executives may feel uneasy with the concept of emergent strategies and may refrain from stimulating them. After all, decades of business thinking and practice have emphasized deliberate strategic planning.
Emergent strategies may be perceived as messy disturbances in a somewhat
ordered world. We grapple with mental models. Actually, deliberate and
emergent strategies are not substitutes but complements. The former are
very appropriate for the "structured complexity" elements of the strategic

landscape, where uncertainty is low, but the latter are indispensable to handle the "unstructured complexity" of uncertain contexts.

Leadership

Leading through the Long Conversation is like raising a teenager. During those challenging years of people's life, parents want their children to make a successful transition to adulthood. Consider the choice of an occupation and lifestyle. To attain sustainable autonomy, a young adult need to choose an occupation and lifestyle that suits his or her personality and skills. Self-discovery implies identifying and trying alternative paths, discarding misfits and further exploring the ones that promise success and personal satisfaction, and finally making their own mature choices.

What should be the parent's role? Children do need guidance along the journey; however, their destination cannot be predefined by parents but discovered by the children themselves. Successful parents concentrate on describing a vision of adulthood as responsible and satisfactory autonomy, providing their children with opportunities for self-discovery, supporting them during setbacks while motivating them to keep advancing, helping them to strengthen their value- base, and encouraging them to (eventually) make sense of their exploration and start making informed choices. This approach can be defined as "involved and developmental." Successful parents are not detached from their children, they are involved. But their involvement is not about living their children's lives, but about helping them to develop into young adults. By doing this, parents create an atmosphere for learning and self-discovery that support a successful transition through this phase of peak unstructured complexity in life.

CEOs face a similar situation during the Long Conversation. They cannot be too "directive," indicating the specific actions to be taken to deepen ES adoption. That would require an omniscient CEO amid great uncertainty, and it will certainly inhibit the ES management team disposition for exploring business value opportunities. On the other hand, CEOs cannot err on the side of being too laissez-faire either; that would risk investing time and resources and getting nowhere. The right leadership approach in an environment of unstructured complexity, as in our teenager example, is "involved and developmental," concentrating on five elements:

- Present a vision of ES adoption that combines greater business value from the ES and deeper integration of business and IT domains within the company.

- Lay a base of guiding values for the process that comprise both learning and attaining the vision of ES adoption.
- Create the environment for exploration and discovery, encouraging key-users from the initial ES adoption phase to examine new venues for value creation, allocating resources and providing incentives to those engaged in the learning process.
- Get involved in reviewing results of opportunity discovery, praising learning from both successful and failed explorations.
- Make sure the process converge by closing nonpromising explorations, structuring learning from successful prototypes, and deploying functionality through osmosis to materialize business value from the ES.

This leadership approach, exercised by the CEO and the ES management team creates the appropriate context for the long conversation.

People

Key users are not only crucial during the initial ES adoption phase. They are also important during Long Conversation. In both phases, key users leverage their unique knowledge and perspective, aligning bi-directionally the horizontal perspective of process and ES configuration with the vertical perspective of intra-area tasks and roles. At the initial phase of ES adoption, the role of key users follows a mechanistic paradigm: they contribute to the design and control of a structured ES implementation plan (which contemplates all expected interdependencies between areas), and take responsibility for executing the plan details that concern their areas. Afterward, they help training end-users in their areas on the ES functionality.

The nature of the pivoting role of key users changes drastically during the Long Conversation. When an organic paradigm is assumed and both the social and technical dimensions of the tech wave are incorporated, key users must change their role from helping to "build, execute and control the plan" to "action-learning and knowledge diffusion." When opportunities for enhanced ES business value are explored, key users participate in a collective action-learning deriving knowledge that encompass and connect both the horizontal process perspective and the intra-unit functional perspective. They become deep masters of the ES functionality. As learning converges, key users play a critical role diffusing knowledge inside their areas and to other areas. Osmosis, growth and adaptation become enabled by the web of knowledge derived from collective learning and the role of an emerging network of key users that create and nurture this organizational learning process.

Dispersing the key users after the initial phase of ES adoption is a huge mistake, a point we have made before. The knowledge that key users usually develop through the initial planning, configuration and implementation of the ES is a great asset that can be fruitfully leveraged during the Long Conversation. On the other hand, some key users are better prepared than others to contribute in their new role of "action learning and knowledge diffusion." CEOs and the ES management team can certainly help key users in this role transition by creating the right atmosphere for learning and discovery; a leadership style we have described as "involved and developmental."

Although we have stressed the role of key users, it is also pertinent to discuss the role of support process and IT specialists. Engaging in the Long Conversation requires from these professionals to work under a "prototype" mindset.[13] Under the traditional formal structured life-cycle approach to systems development, process and IT specialists represent requirements using modeling tools. In contrast, under the prototype approach, support specialists first help users to discover requirements using a flexible development environment.[14] The prototype mindset is less common among process and IT specialists than its formal structured counterpart, not because of a lack of professional training but because it is less used and practiced in corporate environments.

Organizational structure and coordination

Coordinating the collective learning and action that takes place as part of the Long Conversation cannot be accomplished through top-down hierarchical command and control mechanisms. Mastering the ES during the Long Conversation does not happen in the context of a structured master plan. Discovering and exploring opportunities for ES business value require flexible organizational arrangements that foster the experimentation and learning demanded by osmosis, growth and adaptation. Two structural elements, described in Table 5.5, play a crucial role in this context: intra-unit teams and social networks.

Contrasting teams and social networks in the context of ES adoption provides an immediate impression about how they complement each other. The combination of teams and social networks would allow handling of both the narrow one-dimensional perspective of organizational units and the broad multidimensional perspective associated to enhanced ES

Table 5.5 Intra-Unit teams and social networks role in the Long Conversation

Element	Intra-Unit Teams	Social Network
Organizational Scope	Functional or business units	Multi-functional and multi-business
Size and cohesiveness	Small, closed and tight	Large, open and loose
Members	Employees affiliated to functional or business unit	Users across the organization at all levels. Also, vendors, consultants and colleagues
Perspective	Depth of dimensional detail, regarding function, product, market, geography or channel.	Breadth of multi-dimensional interdependences
Paradigm Variety	Low. Social and technological affinity induces shared paradigms among members.	High. Paradigms may clash, exposing conflicts and dilemmas.
Coordination Role	Key user coordinates ES intra-unit work and learning, connecting it to the larger multi-dimensional perspective addressed by the social network.	Key users participate in cross-functional action-learning and knowledge diffusion across the social network, informing it with their narrow intra-unit perspective.

business value. The productivity of small, bounded and cohesive teams is combined with the effectiveness of networks generating multidimensional knowledge by contrasting diverse paradigms.

Creating a synergistic combination between intra-unit teams and social networks requires two elements that cannot be underestimated: skillful key users and effective governance. As suggested by the coordinating role described in Table 5.5, key users, with their dual membership in both teams and networks, function as a connecting pivot for exploration and learning between both fronts. This duality demands great competence for key users to be effective.

Effective governance, on the other hand, recognizes that the confrontation of paradigms across the social network reflects conflicts and dilemmas between unit goals that need to be resolved. Business value from the ES typically results from win-win solutions to these dilemmas. If governance is ineffective, paradigm variety will make it difficult for opportunity exploration and discovery to converge. This is the role of the ES management team, with the participation of the CEO and key users from functional and business units. Key users propose potential opportunities to ES business value as a result of their pivotal role in teams and social networks. These opportunities are evaluated by the ES management team, which in turn commissions exploration experiments, reviews advances and decides about which experiments to cancel or to scale into formal new ES functionality. The ES management team leads this process following the "involved and developmental" approach described in the Leadership section above.

A final comment is in order relating to how this discussion on organizational structure and coordination relates to our emphasis on a socio-technical approach to the Long Conversation. The crucial role of key users and social networks relates to socio-technical system (STS) principles. The ability of key users to connect their highly cohesive and empowered teams with other teams in unstructured ways is a key lever for designing flexible organizations that adapt to uncertain environmental conditions (unstructured complexity). This has been proposed as a principle of STS[15] arguing that flexibility results from supporting lateral (horizontal) interdependences not addressed in the more rigid vertical hierarchical structure. Not surprisingly, STS also highlights the importance of the team leaders' skill set required to enable this flexible organizational design.

By incorporating social networks we extend on the STS principle of flexibility in organizational design through lateral relationships.[16] Social networks help key users to engage in the lateral interdependencies required by osmosis, growth and adaptation, which are both complex and uncertain (unstructured). The openness of social networks is a direct enabler of osmosis that requires transfer of knowledge across porous organizational membranes. Each step in the staircase of ES Growth poses a challenge of multifunctional discovery and exploration building on knowledge derived from previous steps; the broad scope of social-open networks enables the integration of perspectives from multiple functions and/or businesses. Adaptation implies responding to unanticipated environmental and organizational factors for which the organization does not have an established mechanism in place; social networks enable the lateral relationships required to develop a response in terms of ES functionality.

Planning and control

The menu of organizational capabilities we have discussed so far include emergent strategies, involved and developmental leadership, key users engaged in collective action-learning and knowledge diffusion, IT and process support specialist working with a prototype mindset, and open social networks enabling unstructured lateral organizational interdependencies related to ES osmosis, growth and adaptation. Obviously, the traditional mechanistic approach to planning and control characterized by structured project management is a dysfunctional element in this menu. Does the strong emphasis the Long Conversation has on exploration and discovery mean that we should abandon planning and control?

We have argued that typical project management, conceived to handle structured complexity, is not appropriate to manage the unstructured complexity that results from a tech wave penetrating an organization. The combination of complexity and uncertainty is not uncommon in society and organizations; thus, different versions of incrementalism have been proposed by both political[17] and administrative[18] sciences to deal with the issue of how to manage under those conditions. We draw from those sources to propose directed incrementalism as the appropriate planning and control approach to manage the Long Conversation. Its main tenets are as follows:

- Shared Vision: although the journey may not be planned in detail, a shared vision of the destination is the starting point. Vision is not described through perfectly defined coordinates, but as a common aspiration, in this case: to extract as much business value as possible from the ES. The company may not be able to map the details of the Long Conversation journey, but it should have a shared strategic intent of what it wants to get out of it.
- Transition Paths: advancing from the current state in the direction of the vision may take several alternative paths. Osmosis and growth create a blueprint for brainstorming candidate alternative paths for ES evolution within the company. Obviously, some paths may be discarded early because they do not provide promising business value and/or because they entail unaffordable costs or high business and organizational risks. The rest of the alternative paths stand firm as candidates for guiding the Long Conversation.
- Strategic Options: for each candidate transition path, exploration and discovery experiments are defined; they represent strategic options the company is "buying" in order to attain its vision of high ES business value. As with options bought in the financial markets, commitment to these experiments is only exploratory and resources are allocated on a limited scale. The scope of each experiment depends on the supporting political base and the degree of inherent uncertainty. Each experiment is a calculated risk/reward bet; it aims to explore a promising way to extract business value from the ES with controlled economic and organizational risks.
- Option Evaluation and Management: experiments are executed by the relevant subset of key users and intra-unit teams with the help of the

social network. As experiments are worked through, the ES management team evaluates results. Is there real business value that can be economically unlocked? Is it possible to gather enough political support and overcome opposition if this opportunity is fully exploited? Are business, organizational and technological risks manageable? Attractive options may be escalated allocating full resources, while "failed" experiments are rapidly discarded and "gray" experiments are further explored. This also works at the macro level as the result of options evaluation provides insight about transitions paths. Over time, some paths accumulate attractive experiments proving their usefulness as transition paths to the vision, while others are discarded. Action learning at the level of options and transition paths is constantly and dynamically managed by the ES management team, moving the organization forward through successful increments in the direction of the vision.

- The process of directed incrementalism guides experiments based on osmosis, growth and adaptation. It is directed because the vision works as a compass, but it is not guided by a structured project because, in uncharted territory, maps are not very useful.[19]
- Directed incrementalism is consistent with the other organizational capabilities discussed previously. It supports crafting emergent strategies as experiments are put in place, evaluated and adjusted incrementally. It requires an involved and developmental leadership style, involvement being necessary to evaluate and manage options, while developmental leadership is crucial to create a supporting atmosphere for learning and exploration. Directed incrementalism requires a process and technology prototype mindset to conduct experiments. It also leverages the collaborative network of key users engaged in collective action-learning and knowledge diffusion, providing direction and management toward the vision of extracting business value from the ES.

Motivation

When organizations apply a project management discipline in the early phase of ES adoption, two drivers of motivation are typically at work: to reduce pain from legacy systems and to work in an environment characterized by order and structure. When automation and coordination deficiencies from legacy systems accumulate over time, the resulting work-system tend to be dull and stressful, as workers struggle to enforce nonautomated business rules and workflows. The promise of a different work environment in which the ES has absorbed many bureaucratic elements of work, and people can concentrate on more satisfying tasks, is a strong motivator during the initial phase of ES adoption. Although implementing an ES is usually considered a daunting endeavor, facing it using a formal, structured and planned approach motivates many participants, particularly those personalities who value order and discipline.

The Long Conversation approach motivates people in a way much different than working under a traditional project management discipline. Typically, after completing the initial phase of ES adoption, the most painful effects of legacy systems have been reduced or eliminated altogether. In addition, osmosis, growth and adaptation do not prosper in an environment of extreme order and structure. What the Long Conversation lacks in the traditional elements of motivation, it compensates by a new set of motivation drivers: an environment of collaboration, discovery, conjoint design and public recognition of contribution, combined with the satisfaction that results from achieving business value from ES by co-creating a path of small, progressive victories.

The level of participation required by the Long Conversation is demanding and tremendously satisfying at the same time. Collaborative exploration and design that leads to successful business solutions creates a distinctive sense of pride and ownership. Many people enjoy being part of a discovery journey that starts with a vision and constructs the road as it is being walked; indeed, this is what motivates entrepreneurs, and the Long Conversation requires a significant degree of intrapreneurship.

It can be argued that being motivated by the structured environment of project management or the more open atmosphere of the Long Conversation is a matter of fit with personality types. While this is true at some degree, it is also true that most people react positively to the powerful intrinsic motivators that lie at the core of the Long Conversation. Of course, the "involved and developmental" leadership style is crucial to encourage participation from people who at first do not feel comfortable in an environment of discovery and experimentation.[20]

Change management

To be consistent with the set of organizational capabilities we have discussed so far, change management for the Long Conversation cannot rely on compliance based on top-down hierarchical authority. Leaders should not only be in charge of advancing the Long Conversation using directed incrementalism; they should also create the organizational context for successful application of the organic approach embodied by the Long

Conversation.[21] Change management should focus on three fronts: laying the foundation for initiating Long Conversation, and along the journey, building both political support for the process as well as capabilities for flexible discovery and experimentation.[22]

Transitioning from the mechanistic initial phase of ES adoption to the organic phase of Long Conversation as the tech wave penetrates the organization should not be underestimated. Most companies need a deliberate effort to position a phase of organizational experimentation and discovery. Two obstacles should be overcome: resistance to innovation and difficulty supporting a learning exploratory process. Greater value from an ES is extracted when business process and work-systems are deeply redesigned. However, as in any innovation process, the organization's immune system will resist this change. On the other hand, formal resource allocation systems are not conceived to support a learning exploratory process. To overcome these two obstacles, leaders should put their effort in raising awareness and credibility: awareness of the ES business value still unlocked after the initial phase of ES adoption, and credibility that the right approach to unlock that value is not mechanistic but organic.

Initial conversations with senior management and key users from business units and corporate functions should concentrate on raising awareness and credibility. We have presented the arguments for such conversations, and as they are discussed, some managers and key users will reject them, some will entertain them with certain indifference, and still others will embrace them with enthusiasm. The latter represent pockets of commitment, a coalition of managers and key users open to experimentation, learning and discovery. As this coalition marshals human and financial resources, the foundation for Long Conversation has been laid.

Directed incrementalism led by an involved and developmental style demands time from managers and key users. It is easy to become absorbed by the journey and forget about creating the conditions for sustaining that journey. As we mentioned earlier, after the journey has been initiated, two of those conditions are salient: build political support and increase capabilities for flexible discovery and experimentation.

Building political support along the journey is important because the initial pockets of commitment need to be consolidated and escalated as osmosis, growth and adaptation progress. Incremental victories need to be translated into success showcases that support the initial arguments for the Long Conversation and raise political capital, which in turn is to be deployed to gather support and overcome opposition. Supporters become committed as they become involved in the participative forums that guide directed incrementalism. Opposition is dealt with the usual combination of persuasion, co-optation, neutralization and moving through zones of indifference. The combination of gathering support and neutralizing opposition will broaden the coalition base required to sustain the journey.

Another concern of change management during the journey is to deliberately increase capabilities for flexible discovery and experimentation. These key capabilities have been described in this chapter, but leaders need to be conscious that they get strengthened as they are practiced and refined. The Long Conversation may start with a group of enthusiastic managers and key users; however, the capability to lead through an involved and developmental style, or to participate in a collaborative network of discovery, cannot be taken for granted. As learning unfolds, change management needs to nurture and consolidate these capabilities. Distinguished key users should be positioned as champions. This is also true for process and IT specialists that master a prototype mindset. Managers should foster social networks and intra-unit teams by providing slack resources for discovery, and publicly recognizing positive behaviors. Leaders who master the involved and developmental leadership style as well as the governance skills associated to directed incrementalism will certainly become a valuable organizational asset for conducting Long Conversation, not only during the deep adoption of an ES, but also for the development of strategic capabilities in general.

Conclusions

The initial phase of ES adoption typically ends with a significant reduction in the organizational pain caused by the automation and coordination inefficiencies of legacy systems. Despite heavy use of a structured project management discipline, time and cost overruns are usual, and/or the project is terminated and victory declared after budged is exhausted, falling short on the initial expectation of creating business value from the ES.

However, in many cases, managers realize that a new mutual cross-understanding between business and IT people has emerged, which can be leveraged to embark in a new promising phase of ES adoption. The new phase should take a long-term perspective, instead of short/mid-term; it should take the form of an open discovery, exploration and learning process: it is a Long Conversation. In this phase, as managers understand that they are dealing with unstructured complexity, a transition occurs from the initial mechanistic approach to a more organic approach. ES adoption is not a disruption handled via project management to restore normality as soon as possible (mechanistic), it is a transplant handled by socio-technical adaptation (organic).

Our research shows that managers should place far-less emphasis on the time spans of projects. Projects will be created, utilized and sometimes discarded as part of a long-term journey led by key users. There is nothing wrong with the latter case. Projects can be discarded. This is not the same thing as failure. Project failure does not happen when organization has created the conditions for successfully transitioning to a more effective organic approach where deep business value can be extracted from the ES.

The organic approach requires a new set of organizational capabilities for encouraging learning and sharing mastery techniques within the different business areas. Salient capabilities include a collaborative network of key users engaged in collective action-learning and knowledge diffusion, supported by process and IT specialist functioning under a prototype mindset. These capabilities result from leading through an involved and developmental style that creates a supporting atmosphere for learning and exploration. Another key capability is transitioning from traditional structured planning and control to management by directed incrementalism. The ES Management Team should develop the ability to advance, through an uncertain and uncharted terrain, toward the vision of extracting business value from the ES. Transition paths are explored through low-scale experiments in multiple fronts, which are continually evaluated, discarded, refined and escalated as learning unfolds. This process of exploration creates a motivating environment for professionals and managers. However, as any innovative discovery process it requires deliberate change management aimed at gathering political support and nurturing the organic capabilities along the journey.

CHAPTER 6

The next technology wave

Beyond the information technology Remit

"I'm not good with technology," says someone, as she opens the refrigerator. She then pours water in the kettle and returns it to the hob.

"Technology has changed the firm," says the manager in between phone calls. "When I started work, there wasn't any technology," he says as he lifts a pile of forms onto his desk. He starts filling them in with his biro.

"Technology is best left to specialists," says the company director, as she parks her Porsche at the airport. "The less I have to do with it, the better," she says as she catches her flight to Shanghai. When she is there, she will try to finalize a maintenance contract for private jets in China's bourgeoning aerospace market.

"Technology," it sometimes seems, is a term applied to an invention that people find hard to use or understand. If they can use an invention easily or understand it well, it is seen as something material, but unproblematic. In these circumstances, it again becomes "technology" only when it is remarked upon.

The real task of the workplace is to do good work. What matters is how well the collective functions, how well processes are designed, and how well they are carried out. In any kind of complex environment, this necessitates that the skills and insights of many people are engaged. What it all amounts to is that we need to enlarge our view of what Information Technology (IT) is and how we manage it through projects. It is part of the material reality of the workplace, just as the refrigerator in the kitchen. The "official" IT project and its accompanying business case are no more than some kind of accounting convenience. They will get the system in, but they won't maximize the potential of the business. That maximization is a much longer process. It took six years in some of our cases. Hence the drive for learning continues long after the project officially ends. Moreover, our organizations report that eventually they surpass their expectations. It involves a lot of work and quite some pain, but the combination of the functionality of the enterprise system (ES) and the abilities of team means that they start to work in ways that they had not envisaged. It is a new reality. We liken it to buying the future; something that is more than just a bit of useful software and kit. It is also something much harder to reach for and attain. Hence it is vital to understand and optimize how teams learn about IT long after the official project team has closed its office and gone away.

Models of the present and the future

Let's go back to mental models. Remember that we see this concept in many avenues of management and systems theory in particular. The term has been used by many authors, including the great scenario-thinker, Pierre Wack. Its intellectual lineage draws from psychology, for it is an expression of our cognitive limits. We make sense of the world through a model, but that model is never reality. We are constantly vulnerable to drama from outside of its frame. Chris Argyris and Peter Senge are among the management writers who have described the significance of the concept, as well as theorists such as Peter Checkland, Russell Ackoff and Stafford Beer.[1]

We rely on our mental models to manage all that matters to us. You have a mental model of your family; their attributes, likes, dislikes, weaknesses and motivations. But the model is just a model. We are always in peril of not seeing something very important in a situation.

At an overarching level, a failure with models and a willingness to confuse them with truth explains the financial crisis of the early twenty-first century. Economic models were interpreted as trustworthy reality. Several groups saw it as in their interests to proclaim the veracity of the models even if they doubted them for themselves. The outcome of this combining of model and politics was to force populations to spend tomorrow's money to rectify the errors of today.

For now, though, and with crisis still around us, for many firms the main point of the Long Conversation will be that they have sunk investment in ES. In difficult times, they need to tap the value of their investments as thoroughly as they can. They need to act properly to promote infusion and diffusion through the processes of growth, osmosis and adaptation.

The reality is that today, firms need to use their ES better. They need strong team processes and rituals to make sure that people learn about extending capabilities, that knowledge is shared, that it deepens and that all parts of the organization can make optimal use of the ES platform. This is the priority.

Beyond this, the economic crisis is a good reference point for us because it shows the general dilemmas and difficulty of dealing with complex systems. Beyond easy understanding there lie systems upon which we rely but which we cannot fully comprehend, never mind manage. Whatever the experts profess, economics is one such system.

Within each individual firm, we face similar problems of bewildering complexity. Management of technology, of operations, of markets and of strategy, relies on complex, interlocking mental models. No wonder so much is spent on communication! It is therefore important that we understand that our understanding is partial; always partial. This is one of the reasons why we need to grasp the concept of mental models. Another reason is that the relationship between the model and reality is dynamic. We also need to understand this. Our understanding of the world has a partial and dynamic validity. It does not have a stable, fixed validity.

To cope with this, we need the right attitude to our own ideas – a humility clause, if you like – and a constant process of learning, refinement and revision. We also need models and devices that help us think about dynamics in organization. This last point brings us back to the analogy of waves and the models and thinking that we introduced in Chapter 1. Part of your constant learning processes should be, perhaps, concerned with ways of understanding and representing the dynamics of the organization.

Everybody knows the behavior of waves. They rise with energy, and cascade onward in new patterns and shapes. Where is your firm on the wave of technology? Think about it. Think about the major technology platforms on which it sits, and ask yourself how it has progressed in relation to them. Ask yourself about its ES. Is it near the start of the wave, maybe working through the rising pressures of the early project, or is it at some later point, seeking to exploit it and to find new ways of riding its value? What the firm does, how it acts in relation to the technology, should be informed by your judgment. Critically, however, whatever judgment is made, the firm's exploitation of the technology remains a dynamic. Learning must not stop.

ES was popularized through the 1990s bringing integration of information across the functions of organizations. In some ways, we suggest, they are already a wonder of the modern world. They support just about every big business you can name, providing the information that makes sure food supplies reach your local store, that there's gas in your tank and that your salary is in your bank. Not only do ES support our increasingly networked world of business-to-business integration and supply, but to some extent this world has been invented because of the capabilities of ES.

ES is, however, itself a wave. The great accomplishments and controversies of this tide will be set aside as the wave runs out and new innovations are sought. Some of these new innovations are incremental. We see amendments and enhancements to ES and their deployment. Other innovations are potentially radical and disruptive. Maybe the cloud means that firms no longer host their own ES, but rather deploy some instance on some always-accessible infrastructure. In the meantime, as architecture and languages evolve, there comes the possibility of more adaptable and lower-cost systems. More than anything, though, perhaps it is the business models that change. Greater integration means lower-costs of transfer and new opportunities of value in global supply and demand. Surely, the safest prediction about the future is that integration costs will continue to diminish and as they do, myriad opportunities to build information and data clouds will follow.

We foresee:

1. Deepening of ES use among established firms already using the technology and seeking to use it better. This is the subject of much of this book.
2. Growth out to new sectors and extensions into new geographies.
3. Something new, through business model innovation, a disruption or a series of disruptions.

Further growth of ES technology

Walk along the high street of a new town, perhaps in a new country. The chances are that by virtue of a simple, plastic card you can withdraw money and carry out financial transactions on the high street where you stand. Banking systems are highly integrated.

Now try and check-in to two departments of the same hospital. How do you manage? Do they need you to tell them who you are? Do you repeat the same information? Do they need the same paper files?

There are some notable exceptions but by and large, healthcare systems are not well integrated. Imagine being knocked off a bicycle whilst on holiday to see what we mean. Who will help you and what will they know about you?

Even more than finance, healthcare is a ubiquitous need. Where we are, we need it. The same information matters. You are diabetic. I am 44. She is pregnant, and he is already on medication. As we have seen standardization of processes in industry, we can envisage them in healthcare. Basically, every system needs to do the same thing. It needs to access base information about a person, to report on treatments and administrations, and to integrate across to other people and organizations. Questions need to be recorded alongside findings. As with financial systems, different agencies need different degrees of access to systems. Some agencies just need an ID verification. Others need to know a little more, maybe whether you can take penicillin or are allergic to anything. A few need access to the whole record.

The development of integrated healthcare relies on the adoption of ES across organizations or, if not that, then the development of something of similar capability. It is probably the most exciting arena for the growth of the ES; a difficult but important area for the development of standard, out-of-the-box, information technology.

Then, alongside ES in healthcare, one can see it in new markets, a sort of fingertips and sensory system for the reach of globalization. Africa, Latin America and Asia present new opportunities for ES to expand still further into industries that it supports in Europe, Australia and America.

Business model innovation

Innovation is normally understood as a new service or a new product introduced to a market. It is a well-understood but still fascinating area. Introduce a new take-away function to a restaurant and you have service innovation. Introduce a new range of pizza and you have product innovation.

The idea of business model innovation (capitalized as BMI) is less well understood but important to ES and technology, in general. Does a technology somehow allow a business model innovation? If the answer is yes, there is the possibility of competitive advantage.

So what is BMI? The concept was described in a Harvard Business Review article written by Johnson and his colleagues.[2] Alongside Johnson were co-authors Clayton Christensen, the well-known innovation theorist and SAP Chief Henning Kagermann. In short, the idea of BMI starts with the idea of a business model. A business model has four parts to it goes the argument, and innovation can be induced in one or more of these parts simultaneously. The four parts are as follows:

- The Customer Value Proposition, as the term suggests, is what a firm does for a customer, the job it helps them to achieve. If the offering made by the firm fits a job that customer needs doing, then that's the value proposition. The better the job is done, the higher the value. The more important the job, the higher the value.
- Profit Formula is the way in which the firm makes value for itself. It is made up of the following:

- Revenue model or price multiplied by volume.
- Cost structure, made up of assets, direct and indirect costs, and scale effects.
- Margin model, defining how much each transaction needs to cost to deliver net value over the cost structure.
- Resource velocity describing how much revenue is needed how quickly in order to deliver assets and cover fixed costs.
- Key Resources are the people, technology, products, facilities, equipment and brand required to deliver the value proposition to the targeted customer.
- Key Processes – the key are the defined sets of activities that deliver value, allow replication and allow increases in scale.

Understanding business models and then BMI gives a focus to the learning we describe in the Long Conversation. And if learning happens, innovation can happen. Long Conversation is intrinsically a BMI approach.

Waves of disruption

Meanwhile, the world also readies for the replacement of ES as we know it. Clayton Christensen describes it well.[3] One technology is usurped by another. The guardians of the incumbent had not understood the threat. The usurper had looked inferior or different. Once, it had not registered at all.

Christensen wrote his theory focusing on the hard drive industry, noticing how the investments that a firm made in one generation of disk made them more vulnerable to the threat posed by an alternative. As the headlines attached to The Innovator's Dilemma, his original book, put it, this is how you go out of business when running your company well.

The basic idea is that a technology platform becomes a market standard. Firms that sell the technology proceed to maximize efficiency and to develop market reach and share. This behavior is challenged by a disruptor. The point about a disruptor is that it represents an alternative technological paradigm. Typically, it will do something similar for less, extending market reach and access. Initially, however, its functionality is understood to be inferior, appealing only to a niche that the incumbent industry makes a crucial decision to ignore. The dilemma is that this inferiority of performance and niche appeal gives the disruptor a position from which it can develop and mount a blind-side attack on the incumbent.

Think of an image of a torpedo rising from the deep to cut through the path of a wave, and you will sense some of the energy of the disruptor versus the incumbent. This torpedo is however but another wave, a rising jet stream that cuts through the dominant current and then becomes it. It is the new wave; the wave from the deep.

Enlarge the lens from generations of hard-drive and the theory becomes a workable social theory. Think of the garlanded, guilded scribes of the Middle Ages not seeing much appeal in the functional, short and dull outputs of the printing press. Think Stone Age versus Bronze Age versus Iron Age. Move forward again and think of satellite and aerial distribution of video (the television industry) being attacked by internet-based producers and distributors (the You Tube era). Once the internet had looked like a distraction; a place for teenagers to launch webcam productions of themselves fooling and goofing. Later, it began to take major, live sport, to recycle television outputs, and to foster the production and writing talents of tomorrow. The new wave is arriving (Figure 6.1).

In this book, we have positioned ES as the dominant manifestation of business IT as we currently know it. It originated out of the big database systems of earlier decades and their associated applications. Initially concerned with materials requirements planning, the benefits of a standardized approach saw the technology develop out of this application, and then

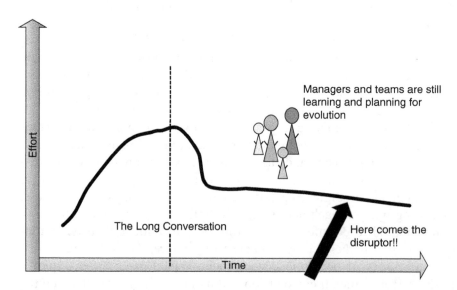

Figure 6.1 The disruption interrupts the wave

across the enterprise. Throughout its long hegemony, it has constantly evolved to meet new business needs, the internet era and to provide Service Oriented Architecture.

The question is, beyond evolution, what's next? What's the revolution? What will the disruptor look like? Is it already available, perhaps in a form that makes it look inferior and only suited to a niche? What will end the leadership of the ES concept over the business IT sector? What is the next ES?

The Cloud

Some people do not like the term "the Cloud." Oracle chief Larry Ellison[4] said it is meaningless, or almost meaningless. For some it is mere marketing jargon; straining to convey something that is already understood by the terms "net" and "web."

We agree. The Cloud is not neatly and precisely distinguishable from existing terms. However, it has value in that it emphasizes the total ubiquity of the web (via wireless plus conventional wired access) and its consequent increased potential as a utility. Portable, and "always-on," networked computing is conveyed the cloud. Within this there is the implication that the cloud makes it easier for different people to collaborate over the same space or application. Think Web 2.0. Then think of a distributed workforce and its members all working and interacting through a common system (European office, Asian office, van drivers, shipping agents, suppliers etc.). Now do you see the cloud?

Moreover, there is nice development of the term "Cloud" as software developers also utilize the term "Cloud Native." This latter term denotes those applications that are specially designed for the cloud and could not achieve their maximum utility without it. Facebook qualifies as cloud native. Imagine how it diminished value if you could access it only through a wired PC and not also through your smart phone. Imagine if friends could not drop messages on to your wall while they holiday abroad.

So, what is Cloud Native to business?

We can conceive of applications that we qualify as cloud native. They would not make sense, or at least would not be as much value, without the cloud. DHL Deutsche Post has talked of delivery systems for convenience stores. Each of these convenience stores is of the "seven/eleven" or "late-opening" type and, for the sake of our illustration, can be imagined as being independently owned or part of a small chain. Margins are thin and volumes have to be maintained as high as possible. Staff costs must be minimized. Every time that checkout staff go to the backdoor to accept a delivery, time is lost at the front door. Queues build at the checkout and sales can be lost. Service reputation can be damaged if a customer is left waiting; next time, they may prefer to go somewhere else. There is also an increased risk of theft. Therefore it is good business sense to have the lowest number of deliveries possible. Yet, on the other hand, it can be good business sense to order from a range of suppliers. This is to achieve optimal pricing and also a wide, novel range of goods. How do we resolve this dilemma? Can we use the cloud? Well, DHL Deutsche Post developed a native application that allows the store to buy from many different suppliers, and to have these suppliers record when the order is ready to ship. This shipment is then reconciled by DHL Deutsche Post so it is able to collect from many different sources but bring the different elements together into as few deliveries as possible. The package company is also an information company, allowing supplier and store to manage key variables themselves, but then to see the whole thing brought together before delivery. It is a classic web application but with the enhanced emphasis of the cloud, we can imagine a fully optimized system. Even the delivery trucks will participate in the information exchange, every component in every part of the order being potentially traceable.

What goes for applications also goes for ES themselves. Why have your own stored on your servers and in your buildings? Why not treat ES as a service to be accessed as a utility from wherever you are through the cloud? Will this utility model be normal in the near future? Is the internal IT team facing its own, mini, blind-side attack from co-location in the cloud?

Flexible systems

Some critics of ES have argued that they are inflexible. They cite high costs of change and the high complexity that comes with them. Typically, these critics argue that the modern business environment is increasingly dynamic requiring increased responsiveness and differentiation from within business. What use are standard and fixed processes in such a context?

Some interesting software theory opens up at this point. In some senses, software can be understood to model an external reality (e.g., an "order" in the real world enacts an "order" in software). This is no passive mirror; however, for the software model also shapes the real world ("produce receipt" passes a receipt into the world). Hence the term proposed by Snowdon[5] and others that describes software as an "active model." The active model both reflects and partially determines its external environment. Effective software architecture, so the argument goes, should seek to faithfully and transparently reproduce the elements of reality that the software relates to, so that it adapts more easily to a changing milieu.

Although largely theoretical, this thinking exposes limits in the current ES paradigm but fits well within the socio-technical emphasis of the Long Conversation. Innovation is unleashed where needs and understandings are more easily translated into software capability. When groups understand best practice but then better it, the software should change to this new cognitive understanding.

Snowdon and his colleagues understand flexibility to be the ability of a firm to respond quickly to changes in the business environment. They give examples of changes such as new market innovations, changed customer demand, altered strategy among competitors, new deals, sourcing and shipment problems. Flexibility is then categorized in terms of the following:

- Type flexibility – arising from the variety of information
- Volume flexibility – arising from the amounts of information
- Structural flexibility – arising from the need to operate in different ways.

Large scale ES have been criticized for their lack of flexibility. They are expensive and difficult to change, the critics complain. We have acknowledged how these standard systems are configurable and customizable. We have also talked of Service Oriented Architecture, a way of constructing and classifying functionality that allows the firm to adopt it and configure it more easily. Yet, still, architecturally, it should be acknowledged that they are rooted in a well-established paradigm. And then, as our historical scribes can testify, the disruptor is little interested in what is well-established.

In general, it can be argued that software methods and languages have evolved constantly so as to provide better abstractions, more manageable architecture and faster development. It is arguable that herein lies the opportunity for disruption of ES. Given data portability – a big constraint – it can be speculated that a new generation of easy-to-adopt, easy-to-adapt process systems will arrive on the market merely through the development of these existing trends. Will starting up a business involve little more than plucking a process from the cloud? Will the development of that business involve little more than the remodeling of that process? If these things do develop, as Snowdon and his colleagues envisaged that they should, will we see a whole new generation of technology emerge?

Events

Stepping back from the idea of disruption for a while, we can see that the ES model of today is still evolving. Event-based ES is a new concept. Effectively, what the concept of "event" constitutes is another class of process. Events are processes that involve other processes in their execution (i.e., they are cross-cutting) but in the pragmatic reality of business operations, are not directly and sufficiently supported by ES. Word[6] gives many examples of events from his empirical studies. They include invoice exceptions, product failures and variance in month-end closing. Common to all of these examples is that they are not in the ideal routine of business. They are not planned for as a normal operational concern of the firm. By identifying and classifying these events, Word seeks to extend the range of ES. Normal processes are now accompanied by events. These might be cross-cutting and occasional variances but as Word's work shows they are still potentially of huge value.

They might also just be disruptive. To speculate in this way, one needs to step beyond Word's concerns and see "event" as a primitive in software architectures, alongside "process" and "data." The concept then extends the kitbag of the system designer, we might want to call her an "active modeller," so that new systems can built out of abstractions we can understand and describe in the real world of business. People can understand "event" as they can understand "process" and "data." Start putting these concepts together in a new way and encoding them in software, and maybe we event something beyond Service Oriented Architecture, something that we might call ES2 or something beyond that.

Conclusion

We took a call from Jumeirah Beach, Dubai. A group of managers had been visiting there and talking about the "Long Conversation."

"We are worried," they said. "Six years!"

"The business case is different," we replied. "You have to fix the business case in a hard-headed way. It has to be realistic. You have to meet the targets it sets and the costs of the system need to be related to the benefits you see there."

"But the benefits do not end there," we repeated. "And there is a lot of talking to do from now on into the future. There is a lot of hard work. This is a new reality."

"Without the Long Conversation everything beyond the business case is intangible. Without the Long Conversation, the risks are greater and the rewards more stuttering or less."

The phone-line between Dubai and Madrid was perfectly clear. There were no crackles or hiss. Early next morning, from an office in the city, we reviewed some slides live, online from Madrid to Dubai. We had a video conference call.

"Innovation isn't stopping," we said. "It is accelerating. This is a new reality."

New technology is vital to society because it drives value, because it delivers capabilities that give firms and societies advantages. In difficult economic circumstances, technology needs to be maintained and exploited, so that firms survive and prosper before the next wave advances. What matters most is big, platform technology – infrastructural advances. One mistake firms make is plotting wave after wave of technology advance without nurturing the value-creating waves in-between. These waves are where organizational capabilities are developed through the Long Conversation of osmosis, growth and adaptation. It can take a long time to extend the platform but in reality, firms need carry on generating value from what they have and working with tactical, intermediate and cheap technology enhancements. Sometime, then, disruption may happen.

Then, again, the model advances.

CHAPTER 7

Final practical guidelines

Over the last decade, we have conducted extensive research on the implementation of enterprise systems (ES). These lessons are valuable in helping organizations, not only to manage expectations and build a more realistic implementation plan, but also to build organizational capabilities that enable firms to maximize business value generated from their information technology (IT) investments.

We argue that implementing ES is a long-term investment that merits a long conversation; a longtime and complex process of learning and shaping. The Long Conversation approach is a new way of thinking about the changes that can take place so that potential value is actually realized. The Long Conversation approach is inextricably linked to "change management." With the Long Conversation, you are building a dynamic of listening and responding.

The application of the Long Conversation model has an important set of practical implications for organizations. We have summarized these into three layers (see Figure 7.1): (1) the business value ladder, (2) the Long Conversation process and (3) organizational capabilities. This works as a cause and effect model. Organizations achieve business value from IT investments by stepping up a ladder of at least three levels: operational, effectiveness and intelligence. The top of the ladder is achieved after a long-term journey composed of the processes of osmosis, growth and adaptation. These processes are based on learning that connects potentiality with reality, desirability with feasibility and concept with context. Then, the Long Conversation model demands a different set of organizational capabilities for top managers (i.e., CEO), key users (i.e., business and functional area managers) and project teams. From a complementary perspective, we can also describe this different set of capabilities according to the multidimensional model of organizations presented in the Figure 5.2.

Let's summarize how the long conversation approach can help you maximize business value from your IT investments.

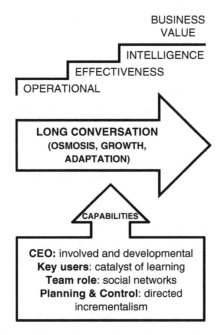

Figure 7.1 Practical guidelines from a three-layer explanation

Managing the Realization of Business Value

When faced with the task of putting together a business case for a new IT investment, it is highly likely that you will be confronted with two main barriers, particularly if the proposed ES cuts across the organization.[1] First, the calculated return on investment (ROI) is insufficient to financially justify the investment, especially as most firms look for a quick return. Second, one of the central questions posed by the Board would be around whether the identified value itself can be realized.

This task necessitates gathering data, conducting interviews and workshops, putting everything together to make the business case. Delivering IT projects on time, within budget, and meeting all technical specifications, does not mean that sought value will be realized even though a strong business case has been made with well-considered ROI.[2] The traditional business case fails to account for changes necessary for the success of ES implementation. This is perhaps due to ignorance of the importance of these changes from those preparing the business case or the realization that their inclusion will increase not only the cost, but also the time required and the risk involved.[3]

We agree with Devaraj and Kohliwhen when they said that the driver of IT impact is not the investment in the technology, but the actual usage of the technology.[4] Our research shows that the most vaunted benefits from large-scale IT depend on expert use and users can only master them only after some time, often in what follows the form of a staircase (i.e., growth). This means that some benefits are repeatedly achieved earlier than others.

Long Conversation: The processes of osmosis, growth and adaptation

Implementing ES is a long and animated conversation involving many players and perspectives. From our research, we know that it takes time, a great deal of time to realize value from your IT investments. Be in no doubt, organizations do not merely learn to live with ES, but also then achieve goals beyond those that they set out to achieve. Organizations redraw the boundaries of their IT projects and pursue learning, team-building and quality.

We have seen that some sense of crisis usually precipitates the redrawing of boundaries in companies such as Charity, Coffee and Engineering. We have also seen that other companies, such as the IT firm, ES project seem to run smoothly because they are looked at as the beginning of a journey rather than the end of a project. Employees work in new ways to relearn the daily tasks they had thought to be routine. By exchanging new insights, new bonds and connections emerge. As this happens, new organizational nodes and networks materialize, and individuals with aptitude in utilizing ES are praised.

As this is the case, then the question posed here is whether firms are wise to pursue tight and ambitious timescales to end projects and to never look back. Would they not be much wiser to recognize the collaborative nature of ES implementation and the resulting organizational development? Adopting successfully the ES is equivalent to transforming the organization from the actual current status to the new desired one. In doing so, osmosis, growth and adaptation, as described in Chapter 3, are three distinctive ways to transform the organization and to achieve business value from the IT investment (see Table 7.1). The processes of osmosis, growth and adaptation require a change of paradigm from managers to conduct the ES adoption like an organ transplant. In other words, a new paradigm is needed to allow the organization to accept the new system and to take full advantage from it. Then, the new paradigm determines a different set of

Table 7.1 The processes of osmosis, growth and adaptation

Long Conversation: The Processes of Osmosis, Growth And Adaptation	
Osmosis	Involves both the implementation of a new ES functionality into additional business functions or processes, and the rollout of a particular ES function already implemented in some part of the corporation into other business units.
Growth	Refers to the development of an enterprise system from a lower or simpler form to a higher or more complex form. This is based on expert use of the system. Enterprise system capabilities are mastered step by step; some are mastered earlier than others. A typical pattern of growth is to master transaction automation and decision support capabilities earlier than coordination and customer service capability. The more aggregated and sophisticated uses related to monitoring performance and process management automation capabilities are mastered after a certain level of maturity.
Adaptation	Means modification and adjustment of an ES in use in a given setting. This factor is crucial in highly dynamic business environments in which organizations frequently have to adapt their business models in order to add value derived from their ES investment.

organizational capabilities, which are different than the ones typically used during initial stages of ES implementation and are imperative to ensure the long conversation leads to success.

Organizational capabilities for Long Conversation

At the early stages of project planning, efforts are directed toward producing a business case that will secure funding for the project. Once the case for funding has gone through, then management may look at implementation issues. Considerations of ES implementation will be driven by those responsible for the deployment of the underlying IT, with detailed project planning considering the selection, development and testing.[5]

Project management is one of the most frequently mentioned critical success factors for ES implementation.[6] Project management tools and techniques (such as project plan/schedule formalization, project scope, quality, cost and risk) have been conventionally argued to help in ES implementation. Typically, a carefully planned and implemented project guides the ES experience. In that, ES implementation is organized as a large-scale project with a beginning and an end. Management of the project is led by a project champion, the project must be formally defined in terms of milestones and deliverables, and monitoring and tracking schedules ensure that deadlines are met.

However, because of the complexity and the multidimensional reality of ES, project management, as described earlier, is limited. Instead of the traditional rigid planning and control, companies eventually will turn to an emergent learning process for their ES implementation. As ES cut right across the organization, ES is not one project but a larger process composed of a number of projects in different localities of an enterprise. This means that one project champion or leader does not correspond to this new reality. He or she does not. Instead, local or decentralized leaders (i.e., key users) take the responsibility for ES mastery, and we have seen the importance of CEOs becoming involved. Although multiple projects can be continuously implemented, the overall ES experience should not be managed as single rigidly planned project. The experience becomes a process for developing employees' capabilities for learning, building and sharing knowledge, solving mismatches and identifying new opportunities for usage.

In light of the above, we are not disregarding the practice of project management, but we are concerned that most practices allow minimal space for an emergent learning process to take place. Therefore, we urge you to consider this approach as much as considering project management itself. Its methods and tools are limited. The entire ES experience should be planned to support the business strategy, while allowing users to develop an emergent process based on learning and knowledge sharing. The initiatives emerging from the learning process should be prioritized and supported by top managers, as well as carefully planning and implementing them based on project management.

What we are trying to get across is that even if the objectives of the project have moved, depending on the changing business needs, or even the discovery of new capabilities in the ES, we believe that by incorporating an emergent learning process, companies are able to respond to these changes. The key is one of getting the balance right between meeting short-term deliverables, and creating long-term learning environment will help you maximize business value from your IT investments.

CEO role: shifting from supporting a project to developing capabilities

Another conventional, but well-received critical success factor is top management support. Their role typically involves supporting the project by clearly defining the project scope, making provisions of resources needed, communicating reasons and consequences of system's adoption, involving users and making decisions when needed.[7]

The CEO's role does not stop there. The CEO also contributes to the greater, emergent learning process mentioned earlier. Top managers are expected to lead, create and facilitate this process and to monitor and control initiatives emerging from it. This suggests that CEOs should create a learning environment for experimenting with ES. All perhaps sounds do-able, but we all know that what matters to top management is meeting deadlines with deliverables. One might assume therefore that CEOs are in the best position to balance the dilemmas and challenges of allowing experimentation whilst meeting project results. Yet, many CEOs find it difficult to get this balance right.

Creating an environment for learning through experimentation can be achieved by establishing social networks within the company. In reference to one of the investigated firms, a key users committee was established during ES implementation, but was also kept post-implementation with an adjusted role. The new role was to create an environment that stimulates knowledge sharing as a result of system usage (i.e., growth and adaptation), integration of areas or business units (i.e., osmosis and growth), and implementation of new projects (i.e., osmosis).

The new role for the CEO is to support the formalization of these social networks and to empower these networks to be part of the mechanisms that manage ES implementation. Taking this role even further, CEOs can participate and encourage top management to engage in these social networks. This will ensure that key users develop new patterns of behavior (e.g., using the system, coaching others, diffusing functionality, taking full advantage of the functionality, and thinking of how to improve processes).

"When new technology is imported from outside the organization, the necessity for observational learning is heightened because there are few or no internally capable persons to practice the art. Senior managers, especially, need to model the behaviors necessary for the entire organizations emulate.[8]"

To ensure the completion of multiple initiatives, CEOs are expected to ensure that learning about the new initiatives continues. Then, the new initiatives are prioritized according to the overall business strategy and current business needs. A learning environment is facilitated where key users manage the implementation of new initiatives through sharing the knowledge created with key users participating in the social network. We have seen that this can happen when the CEO is closely monitoring the evaluation of all initiatives.

In summary, we argue that the right leadership approach that the CEO should play in the Long Conversation model is one we called "involved and developmental" (see Chapter 5). This should concentrate on five elements:

- Present a vision of ES adoption that combines greater business value from the ES and deeper integration of business and IT domains within the company.
- Lay a base of guiding values for the process that comprise both learning and attaining the vision of ES adoption.
- Create the environment for exploration and discovery, encouraging key-users from the initial ES adoption phase to examine new venues for value creation, allocating resources and providing incentives to those engaged in the learning process.
- Get involved in reviewing results of opportunity discovery, praising learning from both successful and failed explorations.
- Make sure the processes converge by closing failing explorations, structuring learning from successful prototypes, and deploying functionality through osmosis to materialize business value from the ES.

Team role: shifting from a project team to social networks

Most experts in change management are convinced of the critical role played by the ES implementation team. Usually, the team is composed of key users, IT staff and consultants in charge of designing processes, configuring the system, and training. It has also been known that having the best onboard, full-time, can be a key element for success.[9] In a typical ES implementation, once the system is up and running, the project team maybe discarded and with it, go the key users. The usual argument here is "there is no need for them anymore."

The Long Conversation approach sees it differently. According to McAfee,[10] enterprise systems are the information systems (IS) that organizations implement to restructure interactions among groups of employees or with business partners. The role of ES team is the development of social networks, in which key users exchange conversations allowing them to create new patterns and behaviors to share knowledge and influence each other toward the ultimate goal of mastering ES.

Social networks should not be limited to key users only, but should also include top management. Because the long conversation approach is inextricably linked to change management, experts in this field support the idea that social network is a mechanism for learning. Mohrman et al. pointed it out in this way[11]:

> New behaviors and schemata may be catalyzed through change-oriented networks such as design and implementation teams. But they take shape in the newly created work units where employees using newly developed processes and IT talk together about how best to get their work done in the new context. As people work in these new task networks, they collectively encounter novel situations and problems and make a myriad of adjustments, large and small, in how they work together. (p. 320)

At this point, one can ask the question: how do companies manage knowledge and learning? The answer is that – in a traditional ES implementation – consultants train employees, showing them how the system works. This traditional training usually takes place shortly before or after the system has been installed. When additional training is required, consultants visit the company concerned and offer support on system's functionality and train users at their desks, without having to move at all. Other ES vendors may approach this differently by seeking to "train the trainers." These are typically referred to as "super users," who then train other users in the same department or division. Throughout this, the traditional perspective on ES implementation focus on transferring information and experience of using the system from vendors and consultants to those who will be using this system for a long time to come.

Evidence from our research indicates that training is essential at the beginning of the emergent learning process, as employees have their first contact with the new system. Traditional training is the single, most dominant element of learning in many ES implementation. Nevertheless, it has been found to be insufficient and sometimes ineffective in getting users up to speed.

Employees need to use the system on a daily basis to carry out their duties. We have seen that companies facilitating knowledge acquisition have been mostly concerned with system usage (i.e., learning by doing). As a result, companies often take an ad-hoc approach to developing new mechanisms to ensure that users learn properly and knowledge is created and shared among them. This can be achieved through the Long Conversation approach, which emphasizes that users create social networks that are the catalysts for managing knowledge and learning.

Social networks, as described in Chapter 5, help key users to engage in the interdependencies required by osmosis, growth and adaptation, which are both complex and uncertain. The openness of social networks is a direct enabler of osmosis that requires transfer of knowledge across porous organizational membranes. Each step in the staircase of ES Growth poses a challenge of multifunctional discovery and exploration building on knowledge derived from previous steps; the broad scope of social-open networks enables the integration of perspectives from multiple functions and/or businesses. Adaptation implies responding to unanticipated environmental and organizational factors for which the organization does not have an established mechanism in place; social networks enable the lateral relationships required to develop a response in terms of ES functionality.

Key Users role: shifting from implementing systems to mastering systems

In the traditional implementation of an ES, key users may determine how the system will affect their tasks and activities; they may recommend detailed system configuration; they may serve as "typical" users during system's testing; and they may be involved in training other users before the system is up and running. Unfortunately, in many ES implementations, once the project is completed, key users are sent back to do what they were doing before ES implementation. Once the installation of the system is accomplished, key users' role cease to exist.

With the Long Conversation, once the systems is up and running the key users lead the additional learning that is needed to fully master the system. Their responsibility evolves to making sure that the company progresses from osmosis, to growth and then to adaptation. In doing so, they are expected to develop the appropriate behaviors, as described in Chapter 4, which enable creating, sharing and spreading ES knowledge. Osmosis, growth and adaptation become enabled by the web of knowledge derived from collective learning and the role of an emerging network of key users that create and nurture this organizational learning process.

Managing the Long Conversation through direct incrementalism

We have argued that typical project management, conceived to handle structured complexity, is not appropriate to manage the unstructured complexity that results from a technology wave penetrating an organization.

We propose directed incrementalism as the appropriate planning and control approach to manage the Long Conversation. Its main tenets are as follows:

- Shared Vision: although the journey may not be planned in detail, a shared vision of the destination is the starting point. The vision is described not through perfectly defined coordinates, but as a common aspiration.
- Transition Paths: advancing from the current state in the direction of the vision may take several alternative paths. Osmosis and growth create a blueprint for brainstorming candidate alternative paths for ES evolution within the company. Obviously, some paths may be discarded early because they do not seem to promise business value and/or because they entail unaffordable costs or high business and organizational risks. The rest of the alternative paths stand firm as candidates for guiding the Long Conversation.
- Strategic Options: for each candidate transition path, exploration and discovery experiments are defined; they represent strategic options the company is "buying" in order to attain its vision of high ES business value. As with options bought in the financial markets, commitment to these experiments is only exploratory and resources are allocated on a limited scale. The scope of each experiment depends on the supporting political base and the degree of inherent uncertainty. Each experiment is a calculated risk/reward bet; it aims to explore a promising way to extract business value from the ES with controlled economic and organizational risks.
- Option Evaluation and Management: experiments are executed by the relevant subset of key users and intra-unit teams with the help of the social network. As experiments are worked through, the ES management team evaluates results. Is there real business value that can be economically unlocked? Is it possible to gather enough political support and overcome opposition if this opportunity is fully exploited? Are business, organizational and technological risks manageable? Attractive options may be escalated allocating full resources, while "failed" experiments are rapidly discarded and "gray" experiments are further explored.

The process of directed incrementalism guides experiments based on osmosis, growth and adaptation. It is directed because the vision works as a compass, but it is not guided by a structured project because, in uncharted territory, maps are not very useful.

Open door

We are confident that the Long Conversation approach will be used by a large number of organizations of all sizes, in both public and private sector across the globe. This approach will be used to maximize the value generated from IT investments and to prevent ongoing practices wasting expenditure. We encourage you to apply this learning to your organization. Going step by step will ensure a sustained IT success.

1. See O. Lorenzo, P. Kawalek, and B. Ramdani, "Long Conversation: Learning How to Master Enterprise Systems," *California Management Review*, 53 (1), Fall 2009.
2. See, e.g., O. Lorenzo, P. Kawalek, and B. Ramdani, "The Diffusion of ES within Organizations: A Social Learning Theory Perspective," in *Proceedings of the 16th European Conference on Information Systems*, Galway, Ireland, 2008; O. Lorenzo, P. Kawalek, and T. Wood-Harper, "Embedding the Enterprise System into the Enterprise: A Model of Corporate Diffusion," *Communications of the Association for Information Systems*, 15 (2005): 609–641; O. Lorenzo and P. Kawalek, "A Model of Enterprise Systems Infusion," in *Proceedings of the European Operations Management Association (Euroma) Conference, INSEAD*, France, 2004.

1   The technology wave, organizations and economic reality

1. See, e.g., C. Argyris, *On Organizational Learning*, London: Blackwell, 1992; Ch. Argyris and D. Schon, *Organizational Learning: A Theory of Action Perspective*, Cambridge, MA: Addison-Wesley, 1978.
2. See K. Craick, *The Nature of Explanation*, Cambridge: Cambridge University Press, 1943. See also an earlier genesis of the idea in Georges-Henri Luquet, *Le Dessin Enfantin*, Paris: Alcan, 1927.
3. See, e.g., P. Wack, The Gentle Art of Re-perceiving, *Harvard Business Review*, 1985.
4. See P. Senge, *The Fifth Discipline: The Art and Practice of the Learning Organization*, New York: Doubleday, 1990.
5. See, e.g., J. Schumpeter, *The Theory of Economic Development: An Inquiry into Profits, Capital, Credit, Interest, and the Business Cycle*, Piscataway, NJ: Transaction, 1982.
6. See, e.g., the work of Ray Kurzweil, *The Age of Spiritual Machine: When Computers exceed Human Intelligence*, New York: Penguin Books, 1999.
7. See, e.g., N. Kondratieff, *The Long Waves in Economic Life*, Whitefish, Montana: Kessinger, 1935.

8. See C. Juglar and W. Thom DeCourcy, *A Brief History of Panics in the United States*, New York: Cosimo Classics, 2010.

9. J. Kitchin, "Cycles and Trends in Economic Factors." Review of Economics and Statistics, Cambridge: MIT Press, 5 (1), 1923.

10. See J. Ettlie, T. Davenport, J. Harris, S. Cantrell, M. Cotteleer, A. McAffe, F. Frei, and V. Perotti, Enterprise Resource Planning Redux. Symposium at the Academy of Management Annual Meeting, Seattle, United States, 2003.

11. See M. Porter, "What Is Strategy," *Harvard Business Review*, Boston, 1996.

12. C.E. Lindblom, The Science of Muddling Through, *Public Administration Review*, Chichester, UK, 1959.

2 Enterprise systems: The technology we already have

1. See O. Lorenzo, P. Kawalek, and T. Wood-Harper, "Embedding the Enterprise System into the Enterprise: A Model of Corporate Diffusion," *Communications of the Association for Information Systems*, 2005, 15, 609–641.

2. See, e.g., R. Kalakota and M. Robinson, *E-business 2.0. Roadmap for Success*, New Jersey: Addison-Wesley, 2001.

3. See, e.g., T. Davenport, "Putting the Enterprise into the Enterprise System," *Harvard Business Review*, 1998, 76 (4), 121–131; O. Lorenzo, P. Kawalek, and B. Ramdani, "The Long Conversation: Learning How to Master Enterprise Systems," *California Management Review*, 2009, 52 (1), 140–166; D. Robey, J. Ross, and M. Boudreau, "Learning to Implement Enterprise Systems: An Exploratory Study of the Dialectics of Change," *Journal of Management Information Systems*, 2002, 19, 17–46.

4. See, e.g., M. Boudreau, and D. Robey, "Enacting Integrated Information Technology: A Human Agency Perspective," *Organization Science*, 2005, 16 (1), 3–18; J. Ettlie, V. Perotti, D. Joseph, and M. Cotteleer, "Strategic Predictors of Successful Enterprise System Deployment," *International Journal of Operations and Production Management*, 2005 (25: 9/10), 953–972.

5. See, e.g., E. Rogers, *Diffusion of Innovations*, New York: Free Press; Cooper, 1995; R. Cooper and R. Zmud, "Information Technology Implementation Research: A Technological Diffusion Approach," *Management Science*, 1990, 36 (2), 123–139; T. Kwon and R. Zmud, "Unifying The Fragmented Models of Information Systems

Implementation," in *Critical Issues in Information Systems Research,* edited by R. Boland and R. Hirschheim (New York: Wiley Series in Information Systems, 1987); C.H. Sullivan, "Systems Planning in the Information Age," *Sloan Management Review,* 1985, Winter, 3–12.

6. See Rogers, *Diffusion of Innovations.*
7. See, O. Lorenzo, "Enterprise Systems: Origins, Characteristics and Importance," IE Business School Technical Note, 2005.
8. See L. Brehm, A. Heinzl, and M. Markus, "Tailoring ERP Systems: A Spectrum of Choices and Their Implications," *Proceeding of the 34th Annual Hawaii International Conference on Systems Science,* 2000.
9. See T. Davenport and J. Short. "The New Industrial Engineering: Information Technology and Business Process Redesign," *Sloan Management Review,* Summer 1990.
10. See Michael Hammer, "Reengineering Work: Do not Automate, Obliterate," *Harvard Business Review,* July–August 1990.
11. See M. Hammer and J. Champy, *Reengineering the Corporation – A Manifesto for Business Revolution.* New York: Harper Business Essentials, 2003.
12. See T. Davenport, *Process Innovation – Reengineering Work through Information Technology,* Boston, MA: Harvard Business School Press, 1992.
13. See, e.g., M. Al-Mashiri, Z. Irani, and M. Zairi, "Business Process Reengineering: A Survey of International Experience," *Business Process Management Journal,* 2000, 7 (5).
14. See T. Davenport, *Mission Critical: Realizing the Promise of Enterprise Systems,* Boston, MA: Harvard Business School Press, 2000.
15. See L. Brehm and M. Markus, "The Divided Software Life Cycle of ERP Packages," *Proceedings of the Global IT Management Conference,* 2000.
16. Ibid.
17. See P. Kawalek and T. Wood-Harper, "The Finding of Thorns: User Participation in Enterprise Systems Implementation," *Data Base,* 2002, 33 (1), 13–22.
18. See O. Lorenzo, "Development of a Model of Internal Diffusion and Infusion of Enterprise Systems," unpublished Ph.D. Dissertation, University of Warwick, UK, 2004.
19. See O. Lorenzo, "Implantación del Sistema SAP R/3 en CANTV Servicios," Caso de Estudio No. 16, Ediciones IESA, 1998.
20. See Davenport. *Mission Critical.*
21. See J. Cederlund, R. Kohli, S. Sherer, and Y. Yao, "How Motorola Put CPFR into Action," *Supply Chain Management Review,* 2007, 1.

3　Biological evolution: Osmosis, growth and adaptation

1. This chapter is based on the findings reported in O. Lorenzo, P. Kawalek, and B. Ramdani, "Long Conversation: Learning How to Master Enterprise Systems," *California Management Review*, 53 (1), Fall 2009.

2. See a detailed biological and chemical definition of diffusion and osmosis in the following source: www.blobs.org

3. This classifying of the use of information systems into different categories is not a new in IS literature. Zuboff, in her pioneering study *In the Age of the Smart Machine: The Future of Work and Power* (New York: Basic Books, 1988) defined two roles for IT: automating and informating. According to Zuboff, when IT automates, it rationalizes work and decreases dependence on human skills; whereas IT informates when it generates vast amounts of information about the underlying business processes and generates a kind of knowledge that allows better participation and relationships. Hence, ES automates business processes so that these processes can be performed with more continuity, uniformity, control and less dependence on human discretion (i.e., ES transaction automation capability); whereas ES informates when it generates information that improves decision-making processes (i.e., ES decision support capability), integration among different business areas (i.e., ES coordination capability) and service to internal and external customers (i.e., ES customer service capability). More recently, Davenport in his book *Mission Critical: Realizing the Promise of Enterprise Systems* (Boston, MA: Harvard Business School Press, 2000) describes several areas of functionality (i.e., actual use) into which ESs may grow. These areas are based on a more sophisticated function for information processing. Hence the informating category by Zuboff evolves toward more advanced concepts related to process management and knowledge management. The ES capabilities of process management automation and monitoring performance capture these more advanced uses as defined by Davenport. Of course, and also argued by Davenport, all these models, classifications, or concepts are not immutable natural laws, as ES is an inherently evolving technology.

4. This framework relies upon Malone and Crowston's definition of coordination as "managing dependencies" (See T. Malone and K. Crowston, "The Interdisciplinary Study of Coordination," *ACM Computing Surveys*, 1994, 26 [1], 87–119). In other words, coordination is seen as a response to troubles caused by dependencies. Typical dependencies that may be handled by ES are those defined

by Crowston as "share resource" and "producer-consumer" (See K. Crowston, 2001 "A Taxonomy of Organizational Dependencies and Coordination Mechanisms," MIT Papers). In the ES context, share resource can be seen as sharing the same body of information between different departments or business units that require it simultaneously. Producer-consumer is concerned with synchronizing activities or processes embedded in a value chain so that the resource required by the consumer is available when needed.

5. The sophistication of this capability has evolved over time. Sophisticated algorithms and operations research techniques have been lately embedded inside the ES. In some cases, this has been possible through the development of bolt-on applications by third-party vendors. MRP (Materials Requirements Planning) and DRP (Distribution Requirements Planning) are examples of management techniques supported by ES. The most sophisticated ES provides automated supply chain management (SCM). E.g., the Advanced Planner and Optimiser (APO) functionality by SAP. MRP/DRP techniques have been developed as sophisticated, computerized planning tools that aim to make the necessary materials or inventory available when needed. The concept originated with MRP, an inventory control technique for determining dependent demand for manufacturing supply. Subsequently, manufacturing resource planning (MRP II) was developed with the objective of improving productivity through the detailed planning and control of production resources. MRP II is based on an integrated approach to the whole manufacturing process from orders through production planning and control techniques to the purchasing and supply of materials. DRP is the application of MRP II techniques to the management of inventory and material flow – effective warehousing and transportation support. (See more about MRP and DRP techniques in A. Rushton, J. Oxley, and P. Croucher, 2001, *Handbook of Logistics and Distribution Management*, 2nd Edition, London: Kogan Page.

6. These three levels have been characterized by using concepts and terms that have been borrowed from (i) P. Bocij, D. Chaffey, A. Greasley and S. Hickie, *Business Information systems: Technology Development and Management*, London: Pitman, 1999; (ii) M. Markus, "Paradigm Shifts – E-Business and Business / Systems Integration," *Communications of the Association for Information Systems*, 2000, 4 (10), and (iii) T. Davenport, *Mission Critical: Realizing the Promise of Enterprise Systems,* Boston, MA: Harvard Business School Press, 2000.

7. The relationship between osmosis and growth was also found by Cooper and Zmud in their study of Material Requirements Planning (MRP)

adoption. The degree of MRP use was related to the implementation and application of more technology's key features.

8. See A. Diaz, O. Lorenzo, and B. Claes, "Exploring the Mechanisms of Enterprise System Value Creation in Supply Chain Contexts," IE Working Paper. This study focused on the mechanisms of enterprise system value creation in multifirm environments through the management of physical product flows. Authors introduced the concept of supply chain-centric enterprise systems to define the combination of systems and functionalities required for supply chain integration. They then studied the inventory practices designed to reduce complexity and uncertainty along the supply chain. Based on an exploratory analysis of 132 companies, they hypothesized that enterprise systems facilitate supply chain integration and that this relation is mediated by the level to which companies adopted advanced inventory management practices. Confirmatory analysis suggested that the development of inventory practices is a capability mastered over time in the period following the implementation of enterprise systems.

9. See T. Anthony and D. Turner, "Measuring the Flexibility of Information Technology Infrastructure: Exploratory Analysis of a Construct," *Journal of Management Information Systems*, Summer 2000, 17 (1). They took the first step toward creating a valid IT infrastructure flexibility construct. Their findings reveal that IT infrastructure flexibility can be expressed in three factors: two related to technical issues and one to human issues. They labeled these factors as "integration," "modularity," and "IT personnel flexibility," respectively. The integration factor is a merger of the dimensions of IT connectivity and IT compatibility. Connectivity is the ability of any technology component to attach to any other component inside or outside the company. Compatibility is the ability to share any type of information with any technology component. This factor suggests that transparent access into all platforms contributes to IT flexibility. The modularity factor is a merger of the dimensions of application functionality and database transparency. Modularity is the ability to add, modify, and remove any component of the infrastructure with ease. IT personnel flexibility is related to the depth and breadth of four types of knowledge and skills: (1) technology management knowledge and skills, (2) business functional knowledge and skills, (3) interpersonal and management skills, and (4) technical knowledge and skills. This implies that technical skills alone are not enough to implement and use IT. One can use Anthony and Turner's dimensions of information systems flexibility (integration,

modularity, and personnel) to argue that enterprise systems are flexible infrastructures for organizations.

10. The presence of adaptation processes of technologies-in-use is not new in innovation and IS experiences. E.g., Tyre and Orlikowski (M. Tyre and W. Orlikowski. "Windows of Opportunity: Temporal Patterns of Technological Adaptation in Organizations," *Organization Science*, 5[1], 98–117) use the term "technological adaptation" to refer to the adjustments and changes following installation of a new technology. In addition, Leonard-Barton (D. Leonard-Barton, "Implementation as Mutual Adaptation of Technology and Organization," *Research Policy*, 1988, 251–267) points out that the adaptation process "is precipitated by implementation misalignments – mismatches between the technology and the organization recognized at the time of initial or trial use" (p. 255). She calls it as "mutual adaptation."

4 Mastery is a long conversation

1. Knotworking represents dynamically changing and distributed collaborative work processes in pursuit of a task organized among actors and activity systems not previously connected. Groups of people, tasks, and tools are mustered for a relatively short period to get some task accomplished. The participants do not usually know each other beforehand and need to be able to quickly create collaborative partnerships that allow them productively to coordinate their activities regarding complex and emergent objects. Historically knotworking type of collaboration has emerged beside the more traditional permanent teams and is associated to the co-configuration type of production. Knowledge Practices Laboratory (www.kp-lab.org); Y. Engestrom, R. Engestrom, and T. Vahaaho, "When the Center Does Hold: The Importance of Knotworking," in *Activity Theory and Social Practice: Cultural – Historical Approaches*, edited by S. Chaiklin, M. Hedegaard, and U. J. Jensen (Denmark: Aarhus University Press), 354–374.

2. See M. Boudreau and D. Robey, "Enacting Integrated Information Technology: A Human Agency Perspective," *Organization Science*, 2005, 16 (1), 3–18.

3. See A. Bandura, *Principles of Behavior Modification,* New York: Holt, Rinehart and Winston, 1969 (p. 73).

4. See Boudreau and Robey, "Enacting Integrated Information Technology."; R. Cooper and R. Zmud, "Information Technology Implementation Research: A Technological Diffusion Approach,"

Management Science, 1990, 36 (2), 123–138; D. Leonard-Barton, "Implementation as Mutual Adaptation of Technology and Organization," *Research Policy*, 1988, 251–267; M. Markus and C. Tanis, "The Enterprise System Experience – From Adoption to Success," in *Framing the Domains of IT Research: Glimpsing the Future through the Past*, edited by R. Zmud (Cincinnati: Pinnaflex Educational Resources, 2000); J. Stratman and A. Roth, "Enterprise Resource Planning Competence Constructs: Two-Stage Multi-Item Scale Development and Validation," *Decision Sciences*, 2002, 33 (4), 601–628; M. Tyre and W. Orlikowski, "Windows of Opportunity: Temporal Patterns of Technological Adaptation in Organizations," *Organization Science*, 1994, 5 (1), 98–117.

5. See A. Bandura, *Social Learning Theory*, Englewood Cliffs, NJ: Prentice Hall, 1977, 160.

6. See T. Davis and F. Luthans, "A Social Learning Approach to Organizational Behavior," *Academy of Management Review*, 1980, 5 (2), 281–290; Bandura, *Social Learning Theory*, 1977.

7. See P. Attewell, "Technology Diffusion and Organizational Learning: The Case of Business Computing," *Organization Science*, 1992, 3 (1), 1–19; A. Bandura, *Social Foundations of Thought and Action: A Social Cognitive Theory*, Englewood Cliffs, NJ: Prentice Hall, 1986.

8. See P. Attewell, "Technology Diffusion and Organizational Learning: The Case of Business Computing," *Organization Science*, 1992, 3 (1), 1–19.

9. See Bandura *Social Foundations of Thought and Action*, p.47.

10. A number of ES work also report these actions as a key part of the ES journey: M. Markus and C. Tanis, "The Enterprise System Experience – From Adoption to Success," in *Framing the Domains of IT Research: Glimpsing the Future through the Past*, R. Zmud (Cincinnati: Pinnaflex Educational Resources, 2000); J. Stratman and A. Roth, "Enterprise Resource Planning Competence Constructs: Two-Stage Multi-Item Scale Development and Validation," *Decision Sciences*, 33 (4), 601–628.

11. The identification of mismatches has been studied in other works: D. Leonard-Barton, "Implementation as Mutual Adaptation of Technology and Organization," *Research Policy*, 1988, 251–267; M. Tyre and W. Orlikowski, "Windows of Opportunity: Temporal Patterns of Technological Adaptation in Organizations," *Organization Science*, 1994, 5 (1), 98–117; O. Lorenzo and A. Diaz, "Process Gap Analysis and Modeling in Enterprise Systems," *International Journal of Simulation and Process Modeling*, 2005, 1 (3/4), 114–124.

12. See O. Lorenzo, *Development of a Model of Internal Diffusion and Infusion of Enterprise Systems*, Unpublished Ph.D. Dissertation, University of Warwick, UK, 2004.

13. ES literature also reflects several examples of this type of actions: Markus and Tanis, "The Enterprise System Experience" .

14. Project deployment (i.e., initiation, implementation and closing) has been acknowledged by literature as an observable activity in ES adoption: Markus and Tanis, "The Enterprise System Experience" ; Stratman and Roth. "Enterprise Resource Planning Competence Constructs."

15. Social Learning Theory (SLT), also known as Social Cognitive Theory (SCT), has its roots in the work of the psychologist Bandura. This theory is fundamentally a behavioral theory of learning from other people (i.e., social learning). SLT encompasses three primary variables: the person (including internal cognition), the behavior, and the environment. The theory proposes that these three variables interact with one another to explain individual actions (i.e., behavior). In other words, behavior is defined by the interaction among a person's cognition, his/her behavior and the environment. See more at Bandura, *Principles of Behavior Modification* ; Bandura, *Social Learning Theory*; Bandura, *Social Foundations of Thought and Action*.

16. See O. Lorenzo, P. Kawalek, and B. Ramdani. "Enterprise Systems Diffusion within Organizations: A Social Learning Perspective," *Forthcoming in Information and Management Journal*. 2011.

17. See A. Aladwani, "Change Management Strategies for Successful ERP Implementation," *Business Process Management Journal*, 2001, 7 (3), 266–275.

18. See Bandura, *Social Foundations of Thought and Action*.

19. See S. Mohrman, R. Tenkasi, and A. Mohrman, "The Role of Networks in Fundamental Organizational Change. A Grounded Analysis," *Journal of Applied Behavioral Science*, 2003, 39 (3), 301–323; L. Bryan and C. Joyce, *Mobilizing Minds: Creating Wealth from Talent in the 21st century Organization*. New York: McGraw Hill, 2007.

20. See Bandura, *Social Foundations of Thought and Action*, 152.

21. Adapted from Lorenzo, Kawalek, and Ramdani, "Enterprise Systems Diffusion within Organizations."

22. Manz and Neck have also defined it as "habitual ways of thinking." See C. Manz, and C. Neck, *Mastering Self-leadership: Empowering Yourself for Personal Excellence*. Englewood Cliffs, NJ: Prentice-Hall, 1999; For Bandura [p. 455], it is defined as "the power of thought resides in the human capability to represent events and their interrelatedness in symbolic form. Whatever fund of knowledge is acquired can be drawn

upon, as needed, to derive new understanding and to guide judgment and action." See Bandura, *Social Foundations of Thought and Action*.

23. See Manz and Neck, *Mastering Self-leadership*; C. VanSandt and C. Neck, "Bridging Ethics and Self Leadership: Overcoming Ethical Discrepancies between Employee and Organizational Standards," *Journal of Business Ethics*, 2003, 43 (4), 363–387.

24. See Bandura, *Social Foundations of Thought and Action*

25. See Bandura, *Social Learning Theory*.

26. See J. Park, H. Suh, and H. Yang, "Perceived Absorptive Capacity of Individual Users in Performance of Enterprise Resource Planning usage: The Case for Korean Firms," *Information and Management*, 2007 (44), 300–312.

27. See W. Cohen and D. Levinthal, "Absorptive Capacity: A New Perspective on Learning and Innovation," *Administrative Science Quarterly*, 1990, 35, 128–152.

28. See Bandura, *Social Learning Theory*.

5   Building organizational capabilities for the Long Conversation

1. Originally, enterprise systems concentrated on providing integration capabilities with moderate flexibility. With the introduction of EAI (enterprise architecture integration), BPM (business process management), and business rule management capabilities, ES have increased their flexibility.

2. Readers familiar with the field of operations research may notice that these statements follow a multiple goal optimization problem with restrictions. First dominant goal is to minimize pain from legacy systems. Secondary goal is to maximize business value from ES. Time and budget ceilings represent constraints.

3. Project management also incorporates other subdisciplines such as procurement, communication, human resource, and integration. The last three relate to the "soft" – people – side of projects. Traditionally, they have emphasized aligning people around the project to execute efficiently and minimize deviations from budget and schedules.

4. Vendors tend to discourage customization because it complicates upgrades. They prefer satellite modules loosely coupled with the ES via EAI middleware.

5. Notice that we have separated ES benefits in two categories: the first one, legacy system automation, reflects a reduction in pain, and it is

associated to the past; the second one, business value from ES superior automation and coordination, reflects an increase in satisfaction, and it is associated to the present and future.

6. Efficiency of the ES adoption process is described as medium-low in accordance with research findings. Lorenzo et al. (2008) studied the adoption of ES in 91 companies in Spain and Latin-America. They found time overruns in 38.5 percent of the projects, and cost overruns in 51.7 percent of the cases. In 16.5 percent of the companies, initial scope was compromised.

7. Strategy represents the purpose of the organization, in particular, the value it intends to create for key stakeholders. Structure describes how people and assets are clustered in responsibility centers according to the nature of work, product offering, target customers, geographical scope, and channels. Business processes refers to the activities to be performed and coordinated to deliver value to internal and external stakeholders. People and culture describe the skills and behaviors of people (including leaders), as well as their values and beliefs. Technology comprises both tangible (equipments) as well as intangible (knowledge) assets that support organizational business processes. Management processes consist of the systems put in place to steer the organization in the direction of its purpose, adapting to the environment and encouraging people toward aligned collective action.

8. We have described the gap between the unstructured complexity of ES adoption and the orientation of the mechanistic approach to handle structured complexity. Most organizations intuitively sense that the gap can be lessened by implementing only a few ES modules and/or by sequencing module implementation over time. However, ES greatest business value potential comes from incorporating several business and functional areas and enabling a superior coordination of the horizontal business processes that connect them. Therefore, eventually facing a high degree of unstructured complexity is inevitable.

9. In the case of a late adopter, at the supply side, the technology may be entering a phase of maturity and standardization. The high-end market of early adopters has saturated and competitive pressures have increased. Thus vendor's strategy turns to addressing the small and midlevel segments with less costly, more standardized versions, emphasizing price and speed of adoption. At the demand side, late-adopters are not concerned with early mover advantage; they see the ES more as a necessity to avoid being left behind, or as a requirement of large sophisticated customers. In other cases, late adopters are companies that have overexploited the life cycle of legacy systems

and have accumulated huge inefficiencies as a consequence. If the demand and supply dynamics of early adopters creates the "searching for tech-driven economic value" theme, in the case of late adopters, it is more like "searching for tech-driven efficiency and control"

10. Socio-technical system theory (STS) has its origin on action-research work performed by Eric Trist and Fred Emery at the Tavistock Institute in London in the early 1950s. While originally focused at the work-system level, it has evolved to be applied at the level of the whole organization and the society. Its main tenet is to search for the joint optimization of the technical and social systems. Scientific management (Taylorism) is biased toward technical concerns such as operational excellence and economic efficiency. On the other hand, the school of Human Relations is concerned with fulfilling the psychological needs of workers and improving quality in people's work lives. STS aims to attain both set of technical and social objectives (Trist, 1981). It is pertinent, to notice that joint optimization is difficult because of the internal tensions and trade-offs between technical and social issues, which are in turn related to conflict of interests between management and the workforce. Also, management's power combined with their preference for Taylorism complicates balanced joint optimization (Maton, 1988). We have discussed both sources of resistance to STS when we concluded that the front-end of tech waves is oriented toward searching for tech-driven economic value. Despite resistance from the traditional organizational paradigm, STS addresses the challenge of designing organizations able to adapt to a turbulent and uncertain environment. To do so, it prefers a simple organization where autonomous groups perform more complex tasks than the traditional complex organization where each worker performs a simple task. In contrast with the typical technocratic bureaucracy, STS emphasizes flexible workers with multiple skills integrated in empowered groups that perform "whole" (as opposed to "fragmented") and meaningful tasks. Leaders of autonomous groups are responsible for horizontally interconnecting highly cohesive groups with one another, supporting lateral interdependences not addressed in the vertical, hierarchical structure. The relationship of Long Conversation with STS is not so much about specific work-system design principles, but about joint optimization of technical and social systems, management of uncertainty (both environmental and internal), and flexible empowered groups working horizontally to drive osmosis, growth, and adaptation of the ES at the back-end of the tech wave.

11. Keen (1997) presents an interesting discussion of how to identify key business processes by combining both strategic and financial perspectives.

12. Mintzberg (1987) discusses emergent strategies as being crafted instead of formulated. He uses the metaphor of a potter: "Virtually everything that has been written about strategy making depicts it as a deliberate process. First we think, then we act. We formulate, then we implement. The progression seems so perfectly sensible. Why would anybody want to proceed differently? Our potter is in the studio, rolling the clay to make a wafer-like sculpture. The clay sticks to the rolling pin, and a round form appears. Why not make a cylindrical vase? One idea leads to another, until a new pattern forms. Action has driven thinking: a strategy has emerged" [...] "Formulation and implementation merges into a fluid processes of learning through which creative strategies evolve."

13. The literature and practice on software engineering and information systems have recognized for a long time the relationship between the degree of uncertainty inherent in users´ requirements and the methodological approach to be followed. Complex systems with low requirement uncertainty benefit from a structured life-cycle approach, whereas simple systems with high requirement uncertainty are better developed through a prototyping approach. Complex systems with high requirements uncertainty (unstructured complexity) usually requires a hybrid approach, where prototyping is used first, and when requirements have been progressively revealed and stabilized by the prototyping process (thus, reducing uncertainty), a formal structured life cycle approach is used.

14. Although ES implementations at corporations are not technically conceived to continually evolve with the help of user-controlled highly flexible development environments, there are several degrees of freedom that can be combined to support a prototyping approach: (a) BPM – business process management – modules have been incorporated into ESs to declare process flows using high-end notations, which the ES is immediately able to interpret and execute, (b) EAI – enterprise architecture integration – modules function as flexible middleware that provide for loosely coupled interconnections of the ES with legacy systems and/or satellite modules developed to capture customized functionality, (c) customization of the ES modules is considered a costly type of flexibility because customized versions are typically not supported by vendors when ES upgrades are introduced; however, if customization has been encapsulated into satellite modules

interconnected with the ES, upgrade compatibility is much easier to achieve, (d) sandbox environments, where new ideas are explored by reconfiguring the ES separated from the production environment, support ES evolution and improvement without compromising the "running" version of the ES; once learning has stabilized, the sandbox version can be put into production after passing quality assurance.

15. See E. L. Trist, "The Evolution of Socio-technical Systems as a Conceptual Framework and as an Action Research Program," in *Perspectives on Organization Design and Behavior*, edited by A. H. Van de Ven and W. F. Joyce (New York: John Wiley, Wiley – Interscience, 1981), 19–75.

16. The popular use of the term "social network" is associated to the very successful web 2.0 applications that have exponentially grown their subscription base in recent years. Although IT social applications are key enablers of social networks, we use the term to describe a set of organizational actors and their meaningful interconnections in an organizational context. Social networks are formed by individual who share knowledge and affinity for a certain theme, in our case the adoption of ES to create business value. For an extended review of organizational social networks refer to M. Kilduff (2010). Readers interested on a more specific treatment of the role of networks in organizational change may refer to Mohrman (2003).

17. Incrementalism in this context refers to formulating and implementing (business or public) policy in stages or increments. In a perfect world, managers would like to have ex-ante perfect information and have enough time to consider objectives and restrictions to formulate an optimal solution, and then design an all-encompassing master plan that puts such optimal solution in place. Unfortunately, reality is messy and uncertain; thus, manager's intention for rational behavior is bounded by its environment and his own cognitive limitations. When managers face unstructured complexity, they proceed incrementally responding to new information and objectives as events unfold. Political scientists proposed "disjointed incrementalism" (Braybrooke and Lindbloom [1970]), as a way to manage uncertainty and bounded rationality in the public sector. Conflicting and changing goals from numerous interest groups plagues policy formulation with high uncertainty. Disjointed incrementalism assumes that aligning stakeholder and creating a shared grand vision is unfeasible, therefore public policy is formulated and executed in increments. Each increment is politically feasible if it is small enough to be accepted by most stakeholders, not rejected by any large one, and if nonsupporters are at worst politically

indifferent. As increments are added, society advances by "muddling through." Disjointed incrementalism is not economically optimal but it is a politically feasible.

18. Managers look at disjointed incrementalism with suspicion because it emphasizes too much political feasibility at the expense of economic rationality. On the other hand, they are very aware of the limitations of bounded rationality and the challenges of high uncertainty on decision making and implementation. Even when organizational politics is a real issue inside organizations, most managers perceive that, in business contexts, stakeholders can be reasonably aligned around a shared vision. It is not a perfect alignment, but it is much more cohesive than its equivalent in the public sector. E.g., agency theory (Jensen [1998]) provides a conceptual framework for analyzing the behavior of agents (stakeholders) and providing incentives toward alignment. In any case, when uncertainty, bounded rationality, and political behavior combine to create a difficult context of unstructured complexity managers have the recourse of "logical incrementalism" (Quinn [1980]). As opposed to disjointed incrementalism, logical incrementalism rejects "muddling through" and emphasizes creating a shared vision that reflects business objectives, although it does proceed incrementally as uncertainty unfold and political support is progressively built. We prefer the term "directed incrementalism" to name this "incrementalism with direction." This term is also being used in the public sector (Rice et al. [2000]).

19. Traditional project management does emphasize mapping the territory before the journey. On the other hand, an emergent discipline called Extreme Project Management (XPM) is being developed to handle complex and uncertain projects (Wysocki [2009]). Consequently, the emphasis is less on task scheduling and more on unstructured human collaboration. Although, XPM is still not mainstream practice among project professionals, it is a promising approach to accompany the Long Conversation at the level of conducting exploratory experiments.

20. Generations that have been raised playing video games and educated under constructivist learning approaches would certainly perceive the Long Conversation as a "natural" approach to manage. When a child is first confronted with a complex video-game, its underlying structure is unknown to him; indeed, he faces unstructured complexity. The child incrementally discovers transition paths to the ultimate goal and adjusts his playing strategy as learning unfolds. As these "new" generations reach middle and senior management positions, we expect many Long Conversations in organizations, not only regarding the adoption

of ES, but also as part of the development of strategic capabilities in general.

21. Beer and Nohria (2000) contrast two theories for change. Theory E exhibits a top-down leadership, focuses on structure and systems, uses programmatic planning, incentives lead motivation, and outside consultants are knowledge-driven. Theory O exhibits a participative leadership, focuses on culture, uses emergent planning, incentives lag motivation and outside consultants are process driven. Clearly, Theory E characterizes the traditional project-based approach used in the initial phase of ES Adoption, while Theory O is consistent with the Long Conversation.

22. This section is inspired by Quinn´s (1980) integrated discussion of change management in the context of logical incrementalism.

6   The next technology wave

1. See, e.g., P. Checkland, *Systems Thinking, Systems Practice*, Chichester, UK: Wiley, 1999; R. Ackoff, *Redesigning the Future: A Systems Approach to Societal Problems*, New York: John Wiley & Sons, 1974; and S. Beer, *The Heart of Enterprise*, New York: Wiley, 1995.

2. Reinventing Your Business Models. Mark W. Johnson, Clayton M. Christensen, and Henning Kagermann. HBR December 2008.

3. See Clayton Christensen, 1998, *The Innovator's Dilemma: When New Technologies Cause Great Firms to Fail,* New York.

4. See, e.g., "Why Larry Ellison Hates the Cloud," You Tube, http://www.youtube.com/ watch?v=8UYa6gQC14o, accessed February 11, 2011.

5. See R. A. Snowdon, B. C. Warboys, R. M. Greenwood, C. P. Holland, P. J. Kawalek, and D. R. Shaw, "On the Architecture and Form of Flexible Process Support," *Software Process: Improvement and Practice*, 2007, 12, 21–34.

6. See J. B. Word, "The Event-Centric Enterprise: A Multiple Case Study Analysis and Theoretical Framework For Event-Centric Business Processes," PhD Thesis, University of Manchester, 2010.

7   Final practical guidelines

1. J. Peppard and J. Ward, "Unlocking the Business Value from IT Investments" *California Management Review*, 2005, 48 (1), 52–70.

2. Ibid.

3. See J. Ward and E. Daniel, *Benefits Management: Delivering Value from IS & IT Investments.* England: Wiley, 2006.

4. See S. Devaraj and R. Kohli, "Performance Impacts of Information Technology: Is Actual Usage the Missing Link?" *Management Science,* 49 (3), 2003, 273–289.

5. See Ward and Daniel, *Benefits Management.*

6. See, e.g., J. Esteves and J. Pastor, J. 2001b op cit.; and Davenport, T. op cit.

7. See, e.g., Davenport, T. op cit.; Esteves, J. and Pastor, J. 2001a. op cit.

8. See J. Ettlie, T. Davenport, J. Harris, S. Cantrell, M. Cotteleer, A. McAffe, F. Frei, and V. Perotti, "ERP Redux. In 'Symposium at the Academy of Management Annual Meeting,'" Seattle, USA.

9. See, e.g., Davenport, T. op cit.; Esteves, J. and Pastor, J. 2001a op cit.

10. See A. McAfee, "Mastering the Three Worlds of Information Technology" *Harvard Business Review,* 2006, 84 (11), November, 141–150.

11. See S. Mohrman, R. Tenkasi, and A. Mohrman, "The Role of Networks in Fundamental Organizational Change. A Grounded Analysis," *Journal of Applied Behavioral Science,* 2003, 39 (3), 301–323.

Anthony, T. and D. Turner. "Measuring the Flexibility of Information Technology Infrastructure: Exploratory Analysis of a Construct," *Journal of Management Information Systems*, Summer 2000, 17, 1.

Argyris, C. *On Organizational Learning*, London: Blackwell, 1992.

Argyris, Ch. and D. Schon. *Organizational Learning: A Theory of Action Perspective*, Cambridge, MA: Addison-Wesley, 1978.

Attewell, P. "Technology Diffusion and Organizational Learning: The Case of Business Computing," *Organization Science*, 1992, 3 (1), 1–19.

Bandura, A. *Principles of Behavior Modification*, New York: Holt, Rinehart and Winston, 1969.

——. *Social Learning Theory*, Englewood Cliffs, NJ: Prentice-Hall, 1977.

——. *Social Foundations of Thought and Action: A Social Cognitive Theory*, Englewood Cliffs, NJ: Prentice-Hall, 1986.

Beer, M. and N. Nohria. *Breaking the Code of Change*: Boston, MA: Harvard Business School Press, 2000.

Bocij, P., D. Chaffey, A. Greasley, and S. Hickie. *Business Information Systems: Technology Development and Management*, London: Pitman, 1999.

Boudreau, M., and D. Robey. "Enacting Integrated Information Technology: A Human Agency Perspective," *Organization Science*, 2005, 16 (1), 3–18.

Braybrooke, D. and C. E. Lindbloom. *A Strategy of Decision: Policy Evaluation as a Social Process*, New York: Free Press, 1970.

Cohen, W. and D. Levinthal. "Absorptive Capacity: A New Perspective on Learning and Innovation," *Administrative Science Quarterly*, 1990, 35, 128–52.

Compeau, D. and C. Higgings. "Computer self-efficacy: development of a measure and initial test," *MIS Quarterly*, 1995, 19 (2), 189–211.

Compeau, D, C. Higgings, and S. Huff. "Social Cognitive Theory and Individual Reactions to Computing Technology: A Longitudinal Study," *MIS Quarterly*, 1999, 23 (2), 145–58.

Cool, K., I. Dierickx, and G. Szulanski. "Diffusion of Innovations within Organizations: Electronic Switching in the Bell System 1971–1982," *Organization Science*, 1997, 8 (5), 543–61.

Cooper, R., and R. Zmud. "Information Technology Implementation Research: A Technological Diffusion Approach," *Management Science*, 1990, 36 (2), 123–38.

Craick, K. *The Nature of Explanation*, Cambridge: Cambridge University Press, 1943.

Cross, R., S. Parise and L. Weiss. "The Role of Networks in Organizational Change," *McKinsey Quarterly*, April, 2007.

Davenport, T. "Putting the Enterprise into the Enterprise System," *Harvard Business Review*, 1998, 76 (4), 121–31.

——. *Mission Critical: Realizing the Promise of Enterprise Systems*. Boston, MA: Harvard Business School Press, 2000.

Davis, F. "Perceived Usefulness, Perceived Ease of Use, and User Acceptance of Information Technology," *MIS Quarterly*, 1989, 13 (3), 319–40.

Davis, T., and F. Luthans. "A Social Learning Approach to Organizational Behavior," *Academy of Management Review*, 1980, 5 (2), 281–90.

Diaz, A., O. Lorenzo and B. Claes. "ERP Implementation Strategies: The Importance of Process Modeling and Analysis," in *Enterprise and Organizational Modeling and Simulation 2010 Conference (EOMAS)*, Tunisia 2010.

Engestrom, Y., R. Engestrom and T. Vahaaho. "When the Center Does Hold: The Importance of Knotworking," in S. Chaiklin, M. Hedegaard and U. J. Jensen (ed), *Activity Theory and Social Practice: Cultural-Historical Approaches*. Denmark: Aarhus University Press, 1999, 354–74.

Ginter, P., and D. White. "A Social Learning Approach to Strategic Management: Toward a Theoretical Foundation," *Academy of Management Review*, 1982, 7 (2), 253–61.

Hammer, M. "Reengineering Work: Don't Automate, Obliterate," *Harvard Business Review*, 1990, July–August, 104–12.

Jensen, M. C. *Foundations of Organizational Strategy*, Cambridge, MA: Harvard University Press, 1998.

Juglar, C., and W. Thom DeCourcy. *A Brief History of Panics in the United States*, New York: Cosimo Classics, 2010.

Kalakota, R. and M. Robinson. *E-business 2.0. Roadmap for Success*. New Jersey: Addison-Wesley, 2001.

Kawalek, P., and T. Wood-Harper. "The Finding of Thorns: User Participation in ES Implementation," *Data Base*, 2002, 33 (1), 13–22.

Keen, P. G. W. *Process Edge: Creating Value Where It Counts*, Boston, MA: Harvard Business School Press, 1999.

Kilduff, M. and D. J. Brass. "Organizational Social Network Research: Core Ideas and Key Debates," *Academy of Management Annals*, 2010, 4 (1), 317–57.

Kim, D. "The Link between Individual and Organizational Learning," *Sloan Management Review*, 1993, 35 (1) Fall, 37–50.

Kitchin, J. "Cycles and Trends in Economic Factors," *Review of Economics and Statistics (MIT Press)*, 1923, 5 (1).

Kondratieff, N. *The Long Waves in Economic Life*, Whitefish, Montana: Kessinger Publishing, 1935.

Kurzweil, R. *The Age of Spiritual Machine: When Computers exceed Human Intelligence*, New York: Penguin Books, 1999.

Kuznetz. S. *Toward a Theory of Economic Growth*, New York: W. W. Norton, 1968.

Leonard-Barton, D. "Implementation as Mutual Adaptation of Technology and Organization," *Research Policy*, 1988, 251–67.

——. *Wellsprings of Knowledge: Building and Sustaining the Sources of Innovation*, Boston, MA: Harvard Business School Press, 1995.

Lorenzo, O. and A. Diaz. "Process Gap Analysis and Modelling in Enterprise Systems," *International Journal of Simulation and Process Modelling*, 2005, 1 (3/4), 114–24.

——. "Enterprise Systems as an Enabler of Fast-Paced Change: The Case of Global B2B Procurement in Ericsson," in C. Ferran and R. Salim (ed), *Enterprise Resource Planning for Global Economies: Managerial Issues and Challenges*, Hershey, PA: Information Science Reference, 2008.

Lorenzo, O., A. Diaz and B. Claes. "Experiencias y Factores de Éxito en la Implantación de Sistemas ERP en España y Latinoamérica," IE Working Paper WP 08–33, 2008.

Lorenzo, O., P. Kawalek and B. Ramdani. "The Long Conversation: Learning How to Master Enterprise Systems," *California Management Review*, 2009, 52 (1), 140–66.

Mansfield, E. "The Diffusion of Flexible Manufacturing Systems in Japan, Europe and the United States," *Management Science*, 1993, 39, 2.

Manz, C., and C. Neck. *Mastering Self-leadership: Empowering Yourself for Personal Excellence*. Englewood Cliffs, NJ: Prentice-Hall, 1999.

Markus, M., and C. Tanis. "The Enterprise System Experience – From Adoption to Success," in R. Zmud (ed), *Framing the Domains of IT Research: Glimpsing the Future through the Past*, Cincinnati: Pinnaflex Educational Resources, 2000.

Markus, M., S. Axline, D. Petri and C. Tanis. "Learning from Adopters' Experiences with ERP, Problems Encountered and Success Achieved," *Journal of Information Technology*, 2000, 15, 245–65.

Maton, B. "Socio-Technical Systems: Conceptual and Implementation Problems," *Relations industrielles / Industrial Relations*, 1988, 43 (4), 869–89.

McAfee, A. "Mastering the Three Worlds of Information Technology," *Harvard Business Review,* 2006, 84 (11), 141–50.

Mintzberg, H. "Crafting Strategy," *Harvard Business Review*, 1987, July–August, 66–75.

Mohrman, S., R. Tenkasi and A. Mohrman. "The Role of Networks in Fundamental Organizational Change: A Grounded Analysis," *Journal of Applied Behavioral Science*, 2003, 39 (3), 301–23.

Montealegre, R. "A Process Model of Capability Development: Lessons from the Electronic Commerce Strategy at Bolsa de Valores de Guayaquil," *Organization Science*, 2002, 13 (5), 514–31.

Newell, S., C. Tansley and J. Huang. "Social Capital and Knowledge Integration in an ERP Project Team: The Importance of Bridging and Bonding," *British Journal of Management*, 2004, 15, 43–57.

Ni, Y. and P. Kawalek. "When the Dust Settles: A Study of Users after Implementation of an ES in a Local Government Authority," *Proceedings of the European Conference on E-Government*, 2001.

Park, J., H. Suh and H. Yang. "Perceived Absorptive Capacity of Individual Users in Performance of Enterprise Resource Planning usage: The Case for Korean Firms," *Information and Management*, 2007, 44, 300–312.

Peppard, J., and J. Ward. "Unlocking the Business Value from IT Investments" *California Management Review*, 2005, 48 (1) Fall, 52–70.

Porter, M. "What Is Strategy?," *Harvard Business Review*, Boston, 1996.

Quinn, J. B. *Strategies for Change: Logical incrementalism*, Homewood, IL: R. D. Irwin, 1980.

Rajagopal, P. "An Innovation-Diffusion View of Implementation of ERP Systems and Development of a Research Model," *Information and Management*, 2002, 40, 87–114.

Rice, J., J. Rice and M. Prince, *Changing Politics of Canadian School Policy*, Toronto: University of Toronto Press, 2000.

Robey, D., J. Ross and M. Boudreau. "Learning to Implement Enterprise Systems: An Exploratory Study of the Dialectics of Change," *Journal of Management Information Systems*, 2002, 19, 17–46.

Rogers, E. *Diffusion of Innovations*, New York: Free Press, 1995.

Rushton A., J. Oxley and P. Croucher. *Handbook of Logistics and Distribution Management*, 2nd Edition, London: Kogan Page, 2001.

Schumpeter, J. *The Theory of Economic Development: An Inquiry into Profits, Capital, Credit, Interest, and the Business Cycle*, New Brunswick, NJ: Transaction, 1982.

Senge, P. *The Fifth Discipline: The Art and Practice of the Learning Organizations*, New York: Currency-Doubleday, 1994.

Senge, P., R. Kleiner, C. Ross, R. Roth and B. Smyth. *The Dance of Change: The Challenges of Sustaining Momentum in Learning Organizations*, London: Nicholas Brealey, 1999.

Soh, C., S. Siew Kien, and J. Tay-Yap. "Cultural Fits and Misfits: Is ERP a Universal Solution?" *Communications of the ACM*, 2000, 43 (4), 47–51.

Swanson, E. B. "Information Systems Innovation amongst Organizations," *Management Science*, 1994, 40 (9), 1069–92.

Trist, E. L. "The Evolution of Socio-technical Systems as a Conceptual Framework and as an Action Research Program," in A. H. Van de Ven and W. F. Joyce (ed), *Perspectives on Organization Design and Behavior*, New York: John Wiley, Wiley – Interscience, 1981, 19–75.

Tyre, M. and W. Orlikowski. "Windows of Opportunity: Temporal Patterns of Technological Adaptation in Organizations," *Organization Science*, 1994, 5 (1), 98–117.

Van de Ven, A. "Central Problems in the Management of Innovation," *Management Science*, 1986, 32 (5), 590–607.

Wack, P. "The Gentle Art of Re-perceiving," *Harvard Business Review*, 1985.

Ward, J., and E. Daniel. *Benefits Management: Delivering Value from IS and IT Investments*. England: Wiley, 2006.

Williams, W., J. Stewart and R. Slack. *Social Learning in Technological Innovation: Experimenting with Information and Communication Technologies*, UK: Edward Elgar, 2005.

Wolfe, R. "Organizational Innovation: Review, Critique and Suggested Research Directions," *Journal of Management Studies*, 1994, 31 (3).

Wysocki, R. *Extreme Project Management: Traditional, Agile, Extreme*, 5th Edition, Indiana, USA: Wiley, 2009.

Zuboff, S. *In the Age of the Smart Machine: The Future of Work and Power*. New York: Basic Books, 1988.

www.ingramcontent.com/pod-product-compliance
Lightning Source LLC
LaVergne TN
LVHW012141040326
832903LV00004B/244